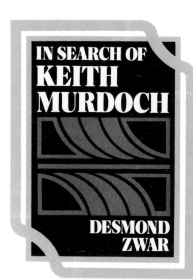

IN SEARCH OF
KEITH
MURDOCH

DESMOND
ZWAR

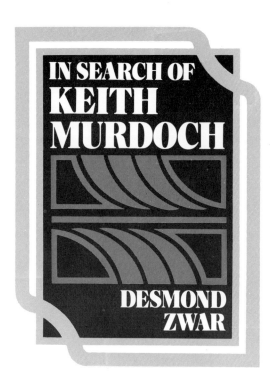

IN SEARCH OF
KEITH
MURDOCH

DESMOND
ZWAR

M

First published 1980 by
THE MACMILLAN COMPANY OF AUSTRALIA PTY LTD
107 Moray Street, South Melbourne 3205
6 George Place, Artarmon 2064

Associated companies in
London and Basingstoke, England
New York Dublin Johannesburg Delhi

National Library of Australia
cataloguing in publication data
Zwar, Desmond.
    In search of Keith Murdoch.

    Index
    ISBN 0 333 29973 6
    1. Murdoch, Sir Keith Arthur, 1885-1952. 2. Newspaper
    publishing — Australia — biography. I. Title.
338.7'61070172'0924

Set in Bembo by Savage & Co Pty Ltd, Brisbane
Printed in Hong Kong

Frontispiece: Keith Murdoch, the young First World War correspondent, working from London. After writing his famous and controversial 'Gallipoli letter', he reported on the war on the European front.

Contents

1 A formidable wall

Had you been in London during the winter of 1909, you might have noticed the tall 23-year-old trudging along Fleet-st., head down, his hands rammed for warmth into his overcoat pockets. Keith Arthur Murdoch would probably have been on his way to a newspaper office for a job interview, hoping, as you brushed past, that it wasn't going to happen again ... that this time no frightful blocking would grip his throat; that whatever force it was that stifled his power of speech and caused his terrible stammer, would relax its hold. *Please God* ...

As you passed, you would have possibly noticed his eyes - large, chocolate-brown, shy, set under heavy eyebrows that sometimes twitched in unison with his mouth as he struggled to unfetter his tongue and the damming up of what he wanted to say. Had you actually greeted him, he may have passed a finger over an eyebrow and his forehead - a gesture which somehow helped relieve the stress. '*H.h.h...ow do you do?*'

'There is a wall in front,' he had just written to his father in a letter he had posted off to Melbourne, 'and I can't stop on this side any longer.' It was the same 'wall' that had obliged him to write a note to Railway clerks at home when he wanted to buy a ticket from Camberwell to Flinders-st. in the city.

Then what was this anxious young man doing 12,000 miles away from Australia, his money rapidly running out, and his only comfort drawn from letters that took six weeks to arrive from Melbourne?

The same disturbing question had occurred to Keith, over and over again. Here he was, standing outside the gates of the 'Mecca' of the English-speaking newspaper world, trying to break in ... an awkward, stammering Australian trying to become part of a professional elite embracing the finest writers in the English language, who had to be - because of their calling - the sharpest of talkers and persuaders.

He had already found himself on the very brink of entering this exclusive club. He had passed a stringent sub-editing and writing test and, feeling suddenly full of hope, had sat down with the editor of the paper for a final interview. To Murdoch's dismay, just when he felt sure his worries were all over, his throat suddenly constricted, his jaws locked and only stultified grunts emerged. There really wasn't much point, said the editor, apologetically, in going on ...

Murdoch made his way back to his bed-sitting room and cooked himself a piece of toast on the fire. Then he told his father with his pen that now he 'keenly felt the determined will-power of the city that shatters the knees of a stranger when he knocks against it. Tremendous strength of mind,' he wrote, 'is needed to force one's way along.'

He would again take from a drawer his list of contacts in the Fleet-st. newspaper world and cross off another. Then to cheer himself up he would glance through the papers of that day and reassure himself: he *knew* he could report and write as well as many of the men who had filled those columns of type. He was a good reporter; diligent, truthful, accurate and honest. He had care and integrity, bred into him from his Scottish Calvinist forebears. He would *make* them want him ...

'Where are you from, then, Laddie?'

'Melbourne, Sir.'

Melbourne. Prim. Starched curtains and half-drawn blinds. Snobbily suburban. Pretentious in some districts, down-at-heel and despondent in others.

'Father in newspapers?'

'No, Sir. He is a Presbyterian minister. The Reverend Patrick John Murdoch.' ... who had gone in the first place to a little church in West Melbourne. Keith had been born in the manse, a terraced house off a'Beckett-st., on 12 August 1885 (according to his birth certificate, but confused in later years by those who had him arriving on the scene a year later).

In case the editor might want to know, he could have told him about Grandfather Murdoch who was also a minister, and who had the calling of the Free Presbyterian Church at Rosehearty, a little herring-fishing village in north Aberdeenshire.

'Mother's father was a minister as well. He h-h-h-had the Free Church at Cruden for some years - that's a parish that takes in the villages of Cruden Bay and Hatton. My parents went out to Melbourne in 1884.'

When they were first invited to sail out to the Colonies the Reverend Murdoch and his wife, Annie, had been assured that the little bluestone church in West Melbourne had a solid congregation of respectable middle-class citizens and that the parish was 'well to do'. But they had not stayed there long.

'Why?'

'Well, the congregation was dwindling and Father hadn't many friends.' ... except for the Reverend James Climie, who had arrived in Melbourne from Aberdeen two years before the Murdochs. He was minister for Camberwell and Burwood East, which was even more well to do, and the church congregation was made up of Scots-stock graziers, dairy farmers and orchardists from around the area.

'After Climie's health broke down,' Murdoch could explain if required, 'Father took over a lot of his services. Climie was only 32 when he died and the congregation asked Father if he would come over to them and become the minister at Trinity Church in Camberwell.'

'Education?'

'Well, Sir, things were not very easy in our house. I have four brothers and a sister, and because there were a lot of needy in the parish to look after, there was not much money.'

No editor would have had the time to listen to his story of boyhood. But it wasn't a happy one. Young Keith had few friends among boys of his own age because of the shyness brought on by his humiliating stutter. (His brothers and sister, even his parents, didn't seem to understand how deeply it affected him.) At first he went to the Camberwell Common school, but the cruel, remorseless teasing he got from the children sent him home in tears. The doctors examined him and said his voice defect was virtually a speech paralysis. Unhappily he agreed to go to a small Grammar school run by two men - one a 'mental and moral philosopher' and the other 'a scientist

2

The Reverend Patrick John Murdoch, a Presbyterian minister from Scotland, who emigrated to Australia in 1884 to take over the parish church in West Melbourne.

Keith Murdoch, aged 20 months. This early photograph was taken on the steps of his father's church in West Melbourne.

with no university degree'. He fared little better there, but made at least a scholastic success of his last school, Camberwell Grammar, from which he emerged after two years as Dux.

When it was obvious to the Reverend Murdoch that Keith did not want to go into the church or to university - or into electrical engineering which he thought was 'the coming thing' - he resigned himself. 'Very well. If you want it that way I'll ask what my friend David Syme can do for you.' Syme was the Scots-born owner of the *Age*, a newspaper as dour as Syme himself. He was more impressed with the fact that young Murdoch had bothered to learn shorthand than with his professed 'insatiable appetite' for newspapers. He made Murdoch an offer which was hardly magnanimous. 'You can bring in news paragraphs and if we use them we will pay you a penny half-penny a line.'

The start Syme had given young Murdoch was probably little more than a polite gesture to an acquaintance; their wives were on 'calling' terms and if the powerful *Age* proprietor should have ever considered he needed a spiritual adviser, he would probably have turned to Murdoch at Trinity Church.

The *Age*, like other daily newspapers, had a team of district correspondents employed on a payment-by-results basis. All, except this new beginner, were well-tried reporters who had once been salaried staff men, but who were now, for various reasons like age and thirst, no longer as useful as they might have been. Syme told the eager young man in his office that he could have the outlying district of Malvern, which Murdoch gladly accepted ... before he discovered that the middle-class residents of that suburb had little time for the newspaper he was going to represent; that their paper was the free-trade, conservative *Argus*. The *Age* was, on the other hand, fiercely protectionist. Murdoch's colleagues had tried Malvern before and made only a miserable pittance on its genteel streets, but that scarcely worried the enthusiastic young newsman. He would take it on with relish. When he got home he told the Reverend Murdoch about it and remarked, 'I notice that Mr Syme does not seem very tidy in his dress. He wears rather cheap ties.'

'Mr Syme,' replied his father acidly, 'can afford to wear cheap ties. You cannot.'

Keith Murdoch was awake early next day to set off for Malvern and tramp its dusty streets. He called on every citizen who might be a source of news. He systematically made himself known to the officials of every local organisation - civic, business, sporting, and, of course, churches. He introduced himself as the reporter from the daily newspaper which had more readers than any other.

He refused to be rebuffed. When he was told that the citizens of Malvern did not believe in the policies of David Syme's newspaper, he answered that this seemed no reason why they should not use its columns to give publicity to the activities of its organisations and its citizens. It was a hard fight at the beginning, made harder because of his speech disability. But as, little by little, he broke through the antagonism of Malvern's leading citizens he found, extraordinarily, that this disability was of help to him. It was difficult to frame a question. At first he was inclined to despair, to walk away instead of persisting. Then, gradually, it came to him that sympathising with the agony his disability caused him, people helped him out, completed the partly phrased question for him, and gave him an answer. Often this answer gave him the news he sought.

He soon found that he could claim official access to the local police court, the munici-

Malvern at the turn of the century - the conservative, middle-class area where Murdoch first worked as a freelance district correspondent for the Age. *(La Trobe collection, State Library of Victoria)*

pal council, the churches, public meetings and sports gatherings. News from these had been given little space in the columns of the *Age* because the paper had previously shown scant interest in a district where it had so few readers. Now Murdoch made his way into the sub-editors' room every day, clutching paragraphs which he sensed were 'news'. The chief sub-editor of the paper was a bearded, formidable character named Jack Stephens and Murdoch made it his business to cultivate him. He told him about the Malvern district, the people he met on his rounds, and the highlights of the typed offerings he had placed on Stephens' desk. The result was that Stephens dealt with Murdoch's copy first, rather than instructing him to ram it on the spike by his elbow like everybody else did. And so Malvern news began to be featured in the *Age*. Reports of happenings in the courts and the progress association made space on the local news pages and now and again Malvern found itself on the main news pages. Prominence given to its activities and its dignitaries pleased Malvern's citizens although they took care not to openly admit it. The circulation clerks told Syme that sales of the paper were increasing rather surprisingly in the area.

Keith Murdoch became aware of the feeling of warmth it gave people to see themselves in an important daily paper; he was intrigued by how much they liked to read what others were doing; that they were interested in what went on in the courts and that they could - through him - evince their pleasure or displeasure at what was being done for them around the council table. Weddings and tea-parties and who attended them - he realised to his profit - were as important as the printed outcome of a thief's fate at the hands of the Malvern magistrate.

Now, each morning, his mother would find him sitting at the breakfast-table in the manse, carefully studying the columns of the *Age*, ticking off paragraphs that were his, then counting the printed lines and jotting down in a notebook their monetary value to him. Over the months the published results of his inquiries had grown tremendously, and so had his bank account. As he had gained experience, he had been given staff reporting assignments in addition to his district work. These 'casual jobs' were paid for by the hour, with a minimum assignment of four hours. As attractive as they might have been, they involved the proprietor in no holiday pay, no sickness allowance; and a 'casual' could be called upon at will, any day or night of the week.

Murdoch was now regarded by the *Age* as a good, reliable reporter with a nose for news and diligence to ferret it out. He was a skilled shorthand writer and a quick transcriber of his notes. Public meetings were reported at length in those days and he was assigned to many important gatherings primarily because of his facility with shorthand. He never got tired of working long hours and soon his efforts put him in a higher-income bracket than his staff reporter colleagues. When, after a few months, he was told he could have a staff job, he was canny enough to refuse; why should he settle for less than he was making now? And anyway, he had bigger ideas. After a year or so more on the *Age* he would make his way to London - all he needed was his steamship fare and enough money in the bank to keep him while he attacked the journalists' dream - Fleet-st. He spent money only on actual living needs, which included a good wardrobe that made him presentable as he went about his calling. By the close of 1907 he had enough put away to go to London for a year: £500 invested in bonds.

It wasn't only for journalistic experience that he wanted to leave Australia. He would tell nobody about it - but his one desire above all was to have his speech disability cured. While he was seeking that remedy he hoped he could also attend the London School of Economics.

When he told the *Age* that he wanted to go, after five years with the paper, Geoffrey Syme, who was in charge of the editorial department, gave him his blessing. (David Syme had died in early 1908.) He wrote:

> I most willingly express my appreciation of the soundness and general excellence of your work . . . although fresh to journalistic work when appointed, your aptitude and ability enabled you to bring what was then a poor district for news its present position of prominence. It is with pleasure that I acknowledge your zeal and industry in the interests of the paper and the thorough satisfaction your work has always given. Trusting the experience you will gain in your visit to Great Britain will be of great service to you and perhaps later on, to the *Age* . . .

Murdoch went to a shipping agent and paid for a third-class steamship passage to London, one way. He now had the encouragement he needed, in black-and-white; Syme - as painfully shy and withdrawn as he was - was not usually given to praise. Above all, in his last sentence, he had said something that Murdoch read and read again: he was offering him security if he failed.

2 Defeat

It did not take long for the thrill of anticipation and the confidence Keith Murdoch had in himself to fade as the P & O liner *Himalaya* drew away from Melbourne. He was uncomfortable with the lack of privacy of travelling steerage in dormitory berths, he was seasick and he was lonely. He was experiencing again what few in the future would ever understand: that while he could be bold and forthright as he approached and questioned strangers for his newspaper work, he could be dreadfully ill-at-ease when it came to private relationships. At 23 he was nervous of mixing with others, and he missed the uncomplicated familiarity of home. It was his first absence from the manse and the commonsense advice and leadership of his father.

He wrote to him on 19 April 1908:

> Dear Father, here I am sprawling in my bunk, ship's rolling still, but we have had lovely weather for crossing the Bight. You have finished Sunday evening service and are either reading in the study - no 'tis 10 pm at home ... it's appalling to think of separation from home and friends for 18 months. You know better than anyone else how firmly attached I am to some of my Camberwell friends. The old associations can never be renewed, but I trust in a few cases friendships will develop in manhood. I wish the time was through and I could return with all the experience obtained.

Then:

> At sea, Straits of Bonifacio. I am dreading these first weeks in London. My stammering has not improved by the trials of the voyage and I hardly feel fit. But I am determined to make a name here before I leave the place, and I'm sure I won't leave even should it cost me every penny I possess until I'm better qualified for good journalistic work.
>
> I know that you have never been keen on my profession and would have preferred a more stable walk of life, nor do you trust press work for any good end. I assure you I would be happy and relieved to give it up. But I see the opportunities and necessities and I shall go ahead and become a power for good. If I consulted my own inclinations I would be in a much easier path than journalism, but I see enormous possibilities ahead. I'm sure I'm following the call of duty.

In the bureau by his bunk he had a bundle of letters which he hoped would get him work in London. There was a brief, formal letter from Alfred Deakin, then Prime Minister, commending him as 'a worthy young newspaper reporter seeking experience abroad'. There were introductions to Presbyterian Church leaders in London and Scotland and to the editors of church journals, the most important of these to William

Fleet street c. 1909. For 18 months, Keith Murdoch tried unsuccessfully to break into this exclusive club, the 'Mecca' of the English-speaking newspaper world. (BBC Hulton Picture Library)

Robertson Nicoll, who edited the *British Weekly*, a paper influencing opinion in the free churches, whose members had seceded from the established Presbyterian Church fifty years beforehand. Great family hopes had been pinned on Nicoll's reception of Keith.

The *Himalaya* docked and Murdoch travelled up to London. He lost no time making an appointment to see the important man.

Nicoll received him with courtesy, and while he regretted there was no immediate place for him on the *British Weekly*, he gave him letters of introduction to several other publications, including the *Church Family Newspaper*. Murdoch hurried off to see this sober organ and to his delight was told he could report some sessions of a church congress and would be paid a casual rate of £2/10/- for three days' work. He had settled in with an aunt whose husband was a family doctor at Mildmay Park, North London, but being with relatives did not diminish the sinking feeling he had that his own home and loved ones were 12,000 miles away. He watched anxiously for the post and when an expected letter failed to come it only increased his sense of isolation. 'I'm very disgusted at not hearing from home this mail,' he wrote to his father in June 1908. 'Surely between the six of you (his mother was on holiday in Glasgow) you should manage a letter a week to me. I have not been very happy because I can't help worrying and fretting.' He enclosed a copy of his journalistic assignment at the congress, but complained that it had been 'shamefully' sub-edited. 'It arrived late and to fit it in and allow room for (the advertisement of) Madam's corsets, they discarded all the brightness of it.'

If he had thought the *open sesame* to Fleet-st. would be through Robertson Nicoll, he was now disappointed. 'He intends helping me, but only indirectly and I am afraid that he does not understand that I'm not fit for really good work ... Everyone here is very good to me. All my introductions have been happily received. I've not had a rebuff except Robertson Nicoll's cold, stern slaughter of some hopes.'

The growing feeling of not being wanted - by Fleet-st., by people who were regarded as influential family friends, and even by his family when the mail failed to bring a letter - soon began to cause him severe depression. Nevertheless he bravely ticked off a list of what he wanted to achieve: 'an immediate, systematic attack on my stammer with an expert recommended by a Harley-st. specialist'; an overhaul of his health problems ('I had a nasty collapse last week'); 'and a good deal of reading and thought'. The stammer was his main worry. It had to be defeated before he could take his part in a profession in which speaking lucidly was as important as writing with clarity.

Then he was in one of his bright moods, and he wrote with hope and some confidence in his destiny:

> I'll be able to learn ever so much here. That's very evident and with health I should become a power in Australia.
> It'll be a struggle and most unremunerative, and so certainly a strain on my purse. I daresay I'll have a pretty bad time during the next 18 months for many reasons, but I face it confidently because I want a struggle. I'm sure things have been altogether too easy for me during all these years ...
> The harder the struggle the better one's experience. The survival of the fittest principle is good because the fittest become very fit indeed.

His stammer wasn't improving much:

> I can speak with effort without hesitation in ordinary circumstances and environment. The suggestion is still there, but I overcome it with effort. In the company of strangers I am still as ever ... I could sit in the study for instance and talk to you for half an hour without impediment, but in the office I would not be quite right.

He was attending the London School of Economics, where he sat in on lectures on sociology, economics and logic, and began feeling ever more keenly his lack of higher education.

> One regret I've always had, Father, is that I didn't go to university. It means that I'm a baby in thought and knowledge. When you offered me the chance, you said: 'It will be a struggle, but we will be willing to make it.' And I thought - with the boys to be educated it was not fair to ask you to make the sacrifice; and besides, I was not very keen on it. I think now it was a mistake, because I know so very little indeed ...
>
> Lastly, Father, I want to be perfectly frank with you about an experience I've had. I suppose it may be called a religious experience. I know that you have always hoped, or had hoped, that I would enter the church's ministry.Well, I've often fancied, or really felt, the call to the ministry and I've always considered it the best work and the highest of all callings. (And it has for a time settled the question.) It has always been ... 'I am not fit' ... I am obviously and completely unfit. Well, sitting in Hyde Park the other day, I felt the call more strongly than ever before. But I may be mistaken as to the nature of the call and as to the promptings - divine, or my own selfish aspirations. I recognise it's a matter to be settled between God and each man in such a position. But I would dearly love to have your advice just now, of course you are 12,000 miles away and I can't get it. I have settled it in my own mind this way - that if by faith, prayer and strenuous endeavour I overcome my stammer and make myself in some measure fitter for the church's ministry, the call will come again, distinctly and undeniably. Tonight I fancy that my path lies clearly to journalism, where undoubtedly great work can be accomplished; but probably in a few days I'll think otherwise.

Another introduction, another electric tramway ride into the West End with hope and anticipation in his heart, another meeting ... another disappointment. This time it was the closest the Fleet-st. door had come to actually opening to the man with 'only Colonial experience which is of little use to them'. Robert Donald, editor of the *Daily Chronicle*, liked him and his earnestness, but saw - as Murdoch did - the obstacle his stammer would place between him and the interviewee. Nevertheless he offered him a job on the sub-editorial desk, editing copy, getting it cut down to the correct size, putting a headline on it. Murdoch had to refuse. 'I had no sub-editorial experience.' On the tram back to North London he wondered 'what it feels like to be without the nervous strain and the half-ashamed anxiety, due to a feeling of being halt and maimed, that possesses me every hour of the day.' Donald had been friendly, and had encouraged the young Australian to send in paragraphs to his newspaper, and two days before Christmas 1908 Murdoch informed his family that he was spending about an hour a day reading aloud and exercising; two hours writing paragraphs for the *Daily Chronicle* and the *Westminster Gazette* ('which usually refuse them') and eight or nine hours attending lectures and reading. 'I'm learning a great deal and feel much amazed and grieved at my absolute ignorance ... the influence of the school is rather anti-Christian. It tends to rationalise which, of course, is not a religion and thus is really a negative.'

Despair sometimes weighed so heavily on him that he became self-critical to an alarming extent and it worried his father who so far away felt helpless to comfort him. Keith had written after one of these moods of self-examination:

> I am afraid, dear father, that I am lacking not only in many qualities of character which go to make a truly useful man, but in depth of insight and in judgment and imagination. I am continually worrying about myself. It's a worry I cannot shake off, although I know I get very near to God every night and that He bears many of my cares. I long for that complete faith which surrenders all into the hands of God. But I sometimes think that such faith is a craven shrinkage from due responsibility placed by God upon man.
>
> At any rate I feel so constantly that I'm unfit for good service that all my work has to be done in an almost haunted and tortured frame of mind. This I fancy comes from two causes: stammering which prompts a constant nervousness and timidity in strange society (and all society here is strange); secondly, ambition.
>
> You'll answer of course, once more, that 'a good servant is required to be faithful and not successful in many things'. But I long for great work and I so earnestly desire those gifts of God, bright children, faithful friends, and a comfortable home. The plain fact is I get fits of beastly depression here which I'm shaking off, but which din into my ears: 'You are of no account; your faith may not even withstand the common temptations of the world.'

London was depressing; the snow was 'appalling'; it brought unemployment to many; it made the streets 'indescribably' slushy, snow-mud lay all over the streets, 18 to 24 inches deep.

He wrote to his father on 28 January 1909:

> London has been wrapt in fog for 48 hours, so dense that drivers have had to lead their horses and traffic has been held up. At noon today a light could not be seen from a greater distance than ten yards. Flaming beacons blaze at street turnings to show that a roadway stretches somewhere behind in the darkness . . .
>
> I walked along the Embankment on Tuesday at midnight and saw a hundred men and women huddled together, bitter cold, dense fog: starvation on every face. Those with sufficient strength left to face Eternity find the Thames and the electric tramways handy . . .

He and Madame Bedake, 'London's best voice specialist', were wrestling with his stammer. 'She fancies I have rheumatism of the throat and that I must sooner or later see a doctor. She thinks . . . I have an abnormally soft palate.'

He wondered, as he thought of the future, if his father still called on Mrs Syme. 'I hope so, because I want the *Age* to take me on to the staff when I return; and it may be necessary for you, if you can with propriety, to speak to Mrs S. about it.'

Parliament opened in early February 1909, and Murdoch went along to see the pageantry. 'We are not allowed in yet, but I got two splendid views of the Royal Procession - gold galore, lovely horses, splendid men and one splendid woman. The high ladies - except the Queen - seemed the reverse of beautiful in spirit. It was all a beastly humbug, but the King is a most useful public servant, and that is the way Australians are going to regard him. We admit no claims of sovereignty or supernatural power.'

12

He had now crossed off all the names on his list of introductions that might have led him into the newspaper world. He returned to the pressingly vital subject of making sure that there would be a job waiting for him when he returned to Melbourne.

> Now for a rather serious matter. I want you to make a short call upon Geoffrey Syme if you can possibly see your way to do it.
> My position now is that I am depending upon the *Age* to give me work when I return. Relying on these promises I'm spending my money on fitting myself for better journalistic work. I want to study at the university here until July and then get experience and travel. But I do not think I am justified in doing so unless assured of a position in the *Age* office after my return. I'm keeping their requirements in view in all my expenditure over here, but must draw in and perhaps return very soon if they will not guarantee me work. Now it is a fair thing that Syme should make some sort of a promise. Of course it is his promise that only really counts. Would you therefore call on him and tell him that I am studying with the view to doing useful press work and that I will be much easier in mind and feel myself safe to proceed if he could hold out certain hope of my work on my return? I hope you agree with me that this is right?

At this time another expert was working on his stammer, 'a Mrs Calwell - a fine woman, and quite genuine. She certainly applies commonsense with a large knowledge of voice production and of the weaknesses of stammerers. But she has not cured herself! And I cannot hope for a complete cure; in fact it seems to be an impossibility. She diagnoses my case as a "mental stammer". You will not understand the point but it is a vital one. You know that most stammerers here do not stammer dumbly. However, I am doing my best and have hopes of at least a very great lightening of the burden. Now that I am here I must completely master this system. I read 20 books at the British Museum on voice production . . .'

The treatment - which cost £15 - did not benefit him at once. He told his father it was too soon to speak of this latest effort: 'I have gone through with the treatment now. It has been a rather heroic measure, forced speaking in a strange way in public and long, dull exercising of the throat, but I think it hopeful. Certainly the temporary relief is great . . .'

He was back in London soon afterwards trudging Fleet-st. from newspaper office to newspaper office looking for work. Unavailingly. London was gradually, but surely, wearing him down. He was living in dingy lodgings in Guildford-st., near Regent Square, a room in a house next to the Caledonian Christian Association which conducted a hostel for young Scotsmen in London:

> The place is OK except for this, that the room I have is next door to the Association's headquarters; that it is over a singing school, and under a drunkard's home; that the bath is next door, and there are fleas in the bed . . . I am paying 25 shillings a week all told . . . The old boy who is at the head of this place, Mr Robertson, a Regent Square elder, is secretary of the association. The boarding house is supposed to help Scots in London. I think it helps many lads but it is wretchedly conducted . . .

The city itself 'disgusted' him,

> although it has a subtle fascination . . . the east is too near to the west; squalor, cold and hunger and depravity too near luxurious culture . . . A shocking feature of London is the immorality stalking the streets.

Flinders street, in 1910, when Murdoch returned to Melbourne from London. (Herald)

As the crocuses bloomed in Hyde Park and the sun shone in London in 1909 he wrote on a brighter note:

> London is looking very well indeed now. The vegetation is very abundant, the residential quarters being studded with parks and squares. I like the idea of these garden squares. They show a lot of foresight in the past of the Londoners of one hundred years ago. This old house I'm in is 210 years old. In the garden there's a well-preserved statue of Queen Anne.
>
> Tell me all about Ivon★ and tell me of your own work. Alec's★ at the age now, as

★his brothers

14

you know, which needs great watching. The forces of manhood are stirring and need only to be directed to useful channels, but you will do it. I have hewn off my moustache ... my razor slipped one morning and Mother insisted that the rest come off too.

It wasn't long before Murdoch's finer feelings were being offended.

I have followed what I have conceived to be the right course and I would value a good talk with you! I hinted before that London upsets me in many ways. One's faith in humanity goes at once; these people are savages ... one's faith in the divine love falters. Educated London declares for materialism and the people in the streets show all the traces of the brutish materialistic evolution. The churches here have little hold except through the superstition of the people. I do not hide from you the fact that I am being daily driven further from the belief in Christ's divinity and that I have hard work in holding to divine love and the divine element in man. I know you would have me, above all things, sincere and you'll have me find a way to the truth through doubt and honest thought. I can write no more about this now, Father, for I have been for days in an agony of chaotic ideas and must just push forward to rational conclusions on which to argue. You will trust me I hope, to think sincerely and as truly as possible. I long to get back to christianity and I feel I shall do so ... I hope I shall.

By the end of April 1909, he finally made up his mind that his crusade to break into the London newspaper world had failed. He would cut his losses and return to Melbourne. Geoffrey Syme had vastly relieved his anxiety by promising him a job on the *Age*. Then, as he began packing, he suddenly saw a chink in the Fleet-st. armour. *He was offered a job!*

It was a position with the *Pall Mall Gazette* which would bring him in between £4 and £5 a week. 'It would mean more canvassing than reporting so for this reason I may turn it down and look for something else.' He went quickly off to the *Gazette* office, and he was received 'very decently, partly on account of Deakin's letter and partly because of good introductions. They say they want a young man to manage a branch office, which they are just opening. They provide office, staff and newsboys and would pay me £104 a year and 10 per cent on circulation and advertisements.' He was to see the managers again the next day.

It was, he realised, possibly his last chance of a job in London. If he had been uncertain before his interview that he would take the job he had certainly decided to accept if the meeting went well the next morning.

But it did not. He failed.

I have rather depressing news, tho' it need not bear you down. I told you of the excellent chance I had of getting good work with the *Pall Mall Gazette*, a paper with a reputation I suppose the cleanest and most honorable in London journalism ... also you know I have been speaking well and had hopes of getting to the end of the trouble.

I passed all the *Pall Mall Gazette* tests, that is the Manager's and the sub-editor's, and then when it got to the final effort, the few minutes talk with the editor, my speaking collapsed and of course we both realised that I would not do ...

It was a tremendous blow.

To be let down so heavily from the heights of optimism was the last straw in many months of disappointments, some of them deeply humiliating. He made up his mind to give up all efforts to work in London.

London does not agree with me. I keep cheery when there is the least excuse for it, but I have insomnia here and indigestion. 'Tis the lack of exercise and the lack of good air, and of good solid work and of any mental and spiritual comfort whatever ...

The more I see of men the more I appreciate the Scot's grip of life and depth and sincerity of vision and especially that applies to one Scot ... Thine, Keith ...

Send me £100 less insurance money ...

He left London early in November 1909, travelling steerage in the Cunarder *Mauretania*. In New York he stayed with a family named McBratney who had been neighbours in Camberwell. He wrote to his father on 30 November:

Steerage in the 'Mauretania' was not as severe as I expected, though bad enough. The worst part was landing at Ellis Island, a small place in the harbour where all immigrants are taken. Yes, that day was the roughest I have spent. We were treated like cattle: big-mouthed filthy officials and heartless bullying doctors bullied us for five hours after which we were chucked ashore at New York, starving, weak and, oh, so angry!

I could have escaped of course, but wished to experience the emotions of a new arrival without money, without friends, without strength. My tender soul was stirred to its depths, and passions and sensations I knew not made my blood boil and my senses reel. A great deal of the misery inflicted here is unnecessary and I mean to tell them so. I was interviewed by the biggest liar of a pressman I have met. The result I enclose ... This remarkable city is given over to rank materialism and industrialism and from many aspects is exceedingly ugly. But it has much to teach in the way of things we must avoid, *eg*, graft and trusts.

In 1910 Murdoch was back in the *Age* building in the heart of Melbourne - but this time as a staff reporter on £4 a week, the standard minimum wage. Salary reviews by Geoffrey Syme brought his pay-packet up to £6 a week by the end of the year.

It wasn't a lot of money considering the long hours worked and the number of stories a reporter had to cover in a day. But his thoroughness, inquisitiveness and his excellent shorthand got him a move to Federal Parliament, then sitting in Melbourne, to report debates. And it gave this complex young man his first opportunity to rub shoulders with his country's political leaders. One was Andrew Fisher, the tall, Scots ex-miner with the broad accent that many Australians found difficult to understand; Fisher and Keith Murdoch's father had been friendly for years. Another Labor man he saw much of was Will Hughes, the clever, sarcastic Welshman who had arrived in Australia rough and who had roughed it into Parliament.

Politicians saw newspapers as their sole communication with the masses and they cultivated the parliamentary reporters. Murdoch, with his insatiable, probing curiosity about men and their political motivation, needed them as much as they needed him. He took Fisher and Hughes, among others, to the Dandenongs village of Sassafras at weekends, where his aunts ran a guest-house and the area impressed Billy Hughes (as he had become known to his distaste) so much that he built a house there shortly after becoming Prime Minister in 1915.

Murdoch was not satisfied that the *Age* was paying him enough; he had been a long time out of work in London and his funds were low; he was worth more money. Secretly, he cast around for 'offers' that might prove to Syme that he was being underpaid. One came. The Sydney *Sun* wanted a Melbourne representative to replace Harry

Andrew Fisher, the tall Scots ex-miner, was one of the first political leaders to be impressed by the young journalist Keith Murdoch. (Australian War Memorial H16066)

Campbell-Jones who was off to London to head a cable service run by the *Sun* and the Melbourne *Herald*. They would pay Murdoch £9 a week to take Campbell-Jones's place. Murdoch went to Syme. He liked the offer, he said, but he would stay at the *Age* for £8 a week. Syme said he would have to decline.

The association between Murdoch and the Melbourne *Herald* that was to become a media phenomenon, began. He moved to a small office in the narrow-fronted brick and weatherboard building at the corner of Flinders-st. and Russell-st. and he hung up his hat . . .

The Sydney *Sun* was at that time the most up-to-date evening newspaper in Australia. Its controlling figure was Hugh Denison, managing director of a tobacco manufacturing business, a man with a reputation as a plucky investor and a lucky racehorse owner.

Denison (born Dixson) entered the newspaper industry almost by accident. In 1908 he loaned £100,000 of the tobacco company's funds to the Australian Newspaper Company, publisher of the *Star*, a Sydney evening newspaper. The loan was secured by a debenture over existing printing plant, which was already subject to a bank overdraft. Within a year the company went into liquidation. Denison took over the paper and its plant, formed Sun Newspapers Co Ltd. with an initial capital of £50,000, put the dwindling *Star* out of its misery, and published a new evening newspaper, the *Sun*. He retained the *Star's* weekly paper, the *Sunday Sun*, which had always had some effulgence.

Hugh Denison, proprietor of the Sydney Sun, offered Murdoch the job which first took him to the Melbourne Herald. They would clash in later years when Denison tried to break into the Melbourne newspaper market. (John Fairfax & Sons)

The *Sun* was an immediate success. Its editorial staff was led by brilliant craftsman Montague Grover, who came over from the *Sydney Morning Herald*, where he was a sub-editor, and included Adam and Delamore McCay, William Redmond and Harold Campbell-Jones, who came from the Melbourne *Argus*.

Denison had no newspaper training, but he had a flair for organising big business ventures and he was a shrewd financier. He had the courage to support anything that carried his wealth if it made profits; but as soon as a venture showed signs of failing to make money he lost his nerve.

Murdoch came to be trusted by Denison and they enjoyed a personal friendship. He was introduced to Theodore Fink, chairman of directors of the *Herald*, and there was an immediate liking on both sides. Murdoch went on working from 1912 until mid-1915 reporting from the gallery and lobbies of the Commonwealth Parliament for the Sydney *Sun*. Then two events threatened to interrupt that service.

Early in 1914 Labour Papers Ltd., a company originally sponsored by the powerful Australian Workers' Union, announced readiness to start publication of a daily newspaper in Sydney. The movement to publish such a newspaper - 'union owned and union controlled' - had started in 1905. The original capital was £100,000. In 1912 this was increased to £250,000, considered then the minimum amount of capital required to establish a morning daily newspaper in Sydney. In that year the subscribed amount of capital was £94,391 (mainly voted from the funds of trades unions) of which the AWU held £30,050. A building had been erected in Pitt Street, Sydney, printing plant

18

The office of the Federal Parliament in Victoria, where Keith Murdoch first rubbed shoulders with Australia's leading politicians as a political writer for the Age. *(La Trobe collection, State Library of Victoria)*

had been bought, and stocks of newsprint were in store.

John Christian Watson, a compositor and the first leader of the Labor Party in the Commonwealth Parliament, was chairman of directors of the company, and early in 1914 he started to recruit staff for the paper, which was to be called the *World*.

Murdoch was among the first reporters Watson approached. He offered him the position of news editor of the proposed paper, ranking next in seniority to the editor, on a salary of £800-a-year and the term of appointment two years. Murdoch was promised in a letter from Watson covering the terms of appointment that 'while it is too early to fix anything definite about the Melbourne paper you can rely upon favourable consideration for the chief position when we extend operations to that city'.

The sponsors of Labour Papers Ltd. were optimistic that, in time, they would publish a daily newspaper in each of the capital cities of the six Australian states. The letter of appointment was dated 23 July 1914. Two weeks later, Australia was at war with Germany and this disrupted any chance of the proposed launching. By October the directors had gloomily decided to shelve their plans until the world's affairs became settled. At the end of 1914 they met again and 'publication or postponement was thrashed out from every angle'. The appointments of the paper's chief executives were cancelled by mutual agreement.

The next interruption to Murdoch's work in Melbourne was to have consequences that would send shock-waves around the world.

3 A terrible decision

As he sat in the press gallery taking shorthand notes of what the fiery Billy Hughes was saying, Murdoch's mind was often straying overseas. Australian troops were already on the water on their way to fight a people most of them had never encountered, and to battle through mud and sands in parts of the world few of them could place even vaguely on the map.

Soon after the war had begun, the British Government informed the Commonwealth Government that an Australian press correspondent would be welcome on that side of the world to cover the fighting. The Australian Journalists' Association was approached to choose a man and it held an election among its members. Charles Bean, a *Sydney Morning Herald* editorial writer, was chosen; Keith Murdoch was only a few votes behind him.

Bean, the AJA choice, a careful, scrupulously fair reporter, was to be paid £600 a year, with a 10/- a day field allowance. His reports would be distributed to newspapers all over the Commonwealth. He was allowed £15 to buy his uniform, was allotted a horse, a batman, and rations for both, and instructed in the use of secret codes for his dispatches. An example of the honesty of the man who was to become official war historian for his country was his first expense-account from Egypt. In a long list that itemised typing paper 4/-, cab 2/-, he explained as a footnote the apparent discrepancy between a half-fare he had charged for the train trip from Cairo to Ishmalia, and the full price of 16/- for the return trip back to base. 'The railway officials in the first case gave me the benefit of a soldier's ticket, but not on the return journey.' Bean said he had also deducted a few shillings from his cable bill because one telegram he had sent home had been 'essentially of a private, urgent nature'. The days of reporters claiming expenses for 'hire of snow-plough', 'services of interpreter' and 'entertainment of Governor's ADC' had not quite yet arrived . . .

Keith Murdoch had found it hard to hide his initial disappointment that he had been so narrowly beaten for the war correspondent's job, but he was soon optimistically looking at new horizons. He had been told privately that the job of managing and editing the United Cable Service in London was his if he wanted it. As a preliminary, he would have to go to Sydney to work in the *Sun* office to learn of that paper's methods and requirements. In London he would succeed Campbell-Jones, who would be coming back as the *Sun* editor. When Murdoch heard of his possible appointment he wrote to his friend Andrew Fisher who had now become Australia's Prime Minister: 'I'll have sole responsibility for the cable service, which is good, but I still have the feeling I should be going to the Front, in spite of your statement that I would make

General Sir Ian Hamilton in London with Winston Churchill in September 1913. His appointment as GOC, Mediterranean Expeditionary Forces, during the First World War would provoke intense and bitter controversy. (BBC Hulton Picture Library)

an indifferent soldier and that (reporting) is my real work.' He nevertheless accepted.

When, on 13 July 1915, the P & O mail steamer *Mongolia* pulled out of Port Melbourne, snapping paper streamers held on ship and wharf, Murdoch was at the rails. He was 30. He was heading for London again; but this time with an assurance that had been absent seven years before. Now he would no longer be walking into newspaper offices cap in hand. He would be working *in* Fleet-st., if maybe technically not part of its operation, and his office would be in the building that housed the most prestigious newspaper of them all - *The Times*.

Down below in his cabin, Murdoch had carefully put away a bundle of correspondence which would introduce him to the new world he was about to penetrate. In a drawer were several formal letters: one from Fisher introduced him 'to whom it may concern' as a 'well-known journalist of Melbourne who was to undertake important duties in connection with his profession', adding, somewhat mysteriously, that 'Mr Murdoch is also undertaking certain inquiries for the Government of the Commonwealth in the Mediterranean theatre of war'.

Senator George Pearce, Australia's Defence Minister, writing on stiffened card, made this 'undertaking' a little clearer in his letter to General Sir Ian Hamilton, GOC at Gallipoli:

A family photograph of three of the four Murdoch brothers: (from left) Ivon, Keith and Alan.

Dear Sir Ian Hamilton,
Mr Keith Murdoch, pressman of Sydney and Melbourne, is on his way to London to fill an appointment there and has been asked by this government to make certain inquiries in connection with postal facilities at the Base in Egypt. It might just happen that circumstances will favour him to the extent of meeting yourself and, in case this should be so, I have much pleasure in giving him this letter of introduction.

Murdoch had undertaken what appears, in modern terms, a peculiar mission for a newspaperman. He was to conduct an investigation, not for his papers, but for his government.

One of the anguishing effects of warfare was the drain on the spirit of both soldier and relatives at home through the uncertainties of mail distribution. Parents, wives and children could wait in vain for news of their loved one without knowing for weeks whether he had been ill or hurt; or for that matter *where* he was. They dreaded the knock on the door or the telephone ring, because either could bring the telegraphic news that he was wounded, missing or dead. For the man at the Front the mail problem was as bad; how were the kids? Was the wife coping? Was Dad's heart still OK? No mail for many days could sap a man's will to danger point.

So it was in Egypt and on Gallipoli in 1915. There was a mail problem. Communications to and from Australian troops slogging it out in the desert and on the beaches had been snarled up. There were allegations of graft involving monies telegraphed from

Australian soldiers at the Front, through the Anglo-Egyptian Bank and Thomas Cook and Sons. Money sent from home had, on occasions, been collected by some other person than the soldier for whom it was intended.

Now reporter-investigator Murdoch, who was to be paid £25 for his trouble, read the terms of reference clearly set out by T.A. Trumble (brother of the cricketing Trumbles), who was acting secretary of the Commonwealth Department of Defence. Trumble said Murdoch would have the following official task:

> That you furnish a report upon the following matters, together with any suggestion for improvement:
> 1: Arrangements for the receipt and delivery of letters, papers and parcels to and from members of the Australian Imperial Force.
> 2: Arrangements for the receipt and delivery of cablegrams to and from members of the Australian Imperial Force.
> 3: Arrangements for notification to the Department in Australia of disposition of wounded to hospitals.
>
> In addition to the matters mentioned in my letter (of 2 July) the Minister would be glad if you would ascertain and report what measures are taken by the Anglo-Egyptian Bank and Thomas Cook and Sons to ensure that remittances made through them to members of the Australian Imperial Force by persons in Australia are paid to the individual whom the sender intends to receive same and not to some unauthorised person. You are aware that rumours are current here of frauds being worked by persons in Egypt in connection with cable remittances.

The Dardanelles: '... broken, rough, scrubby country, full of gullies and sharp ridges ... all within easy range of the guns of the Turkish forts at the Narrows.' (National Library of Australia)

Why send a reporter and not a bureaucrat to sort it all out? 'Many complaints,' explained Trumble, 'have been made to the Minister who feels that a report from some person unconnected with the Forces would tend to allay the existing public uneasiness on these matters.'

Murdoch arrived in Cairo and started his inquiries within hours of settling in. Making his way through the cacophony of pyjama-clad Arabs offering cabs, drinks (and sometimes their sisters) he went to see the senior officers at the Australian training base. He told them he was impatient to get to Gallipoli to further his inquiries and to incidentally send back dispatches from the Front. They advised him to write directly to General Sir Ian Hamilton for permission. On the evening of 17 August 1915 he wrote:

> Dear Sir,
> On the advice of Brigadier-General Legge I beg to request permission to visit Anzac.
>   I am proceeding from Melbourne to London to take up the position of managing editor of the Australian news cable service in connection with the London *Times* and at the Commonwealth Government's request am enquiring into mail arrangements, disposition of wounded and various matters in Egypt in connection with our Australian Forces. I find it impossible to make a complete report upon changes that have been suggested here until I have a better knowledge of the system pursued at base Y, and on the Mainland, and I beg of you, therefore, to permit me to visit these places. I should like to go across in only a semi-official capacity, so that I might record censored impressions in the London and Australian newspapers I represent, but any conditions you impose I should, of course, faithfully observe . . .
>   May I add that I had the honour of meeting you at the Melbourne Town Hall, and wrote fully of your visit in the Sydney *Sun* and Melbourne *Punch*; also may I say that my anxiety as an Australian to visit the sacred shores of Gallipoli while our army is there, is intense . . .

Hamilton sat in his tent and read Murdoch's letter with mixed feelings. He was quite unimpressed with having been 'written up' in *Punch*; and later at a Royal Commission said he thought the letter was 'wheedling'. Nevertheless he agreed to allow the Australian to come across and cabled: 'This cable is your authority to come to GHQ at once whence you will be sent to Anzac: CGS., Medforce.'

Just a week later Murdoch landed on the island of Imbros, where the Army headquarters and the press camp were established. The spirit in the tent village was low; there had been heavy fighting during a second attempt to seize the vital heights and it had failed. He was taken over to Hamilton's tent where the slight man with the moustache greeted him courteously and asked him to outline his mail-investigation mission. Murdoch asked Hamilton if he could go across to Anzac for a few days; the general agreed. Murdoch signed while he was there the official form of declaration that was required to be made by all war correspondents:

> I, the undersigned, do hereby solemnly undertake to follow in every particular the rules issued by the Commander-in-Chief through the Chief Field Censor, relative to correspondence concerning the forces in the field, and bind myself not to attempt to correspond by any other route or by any other means than that officially sanctioned.

That evening Hamilton jotted down in his diary that he saw the Australian as 'a sensible, well-spoken man with dark eyes', who said his mind was a blank about soldiers and soldiering, 'and made me uncomfortable by an elaborate explanation of why his duty to Australia could be better done with a pen than with a rifle'.

Murdoch was taken the rounds and met every officer of importance, renewing acquaintance with several he had known in Melbourne. Charles Bean gave him a warm welcome and escorted him to the war correspondents' camp. Charles ('C.P.') Smith of the Melbourne *Argus* greeted him, and so did Philip Schuler of the *Age*.

Then he was introduced to English correspondent Ellis Ashmead-Bartlett, who was representing the Fleet-st. newspapers. Bartlett, a slim man wearing a greenish hat and crumpled Army uniform, quickly drew the Australian aside and told him his views on what was going on at Anzac. Bartlett was a plucky man (wrote Charlie Bean), 'but doesn't believe in exposing himself more than is necessary to get the story he wants. He lives like a king ... he couldn't think of putting up with the sort of discomfort that satisfies some of us'.

A brilliant, entertaining conversationalist, Bartlett had no qualms about telling those at the press centre he had gone through the bankruptcy court 'a number of times'. 'He works tremendously hard,' said the admiring Bean, 'and his stuff is easily the most vivid written by any war correspondent today.' But he had one glaring fault, which to Bean was a cardinal journalistic sin: he *exaggerated*. 'He gives the spirit of the thing,' scribbled Bean in his small notebook, 'but if he were asked "Did a shout really go up from a thousand throats that the hill was ours?" he would have to say "No. It didn't." Or if asked: "Did the New Zealanders really club their rifles and kill three men at once?" or "Did the first battle of Anzac really end with a flash of bayonets all along the line ... a charge ... and the rolling back of the Turkish attack?" he would have to say, "Well no, as a matter of fact it didn't occur." '

'And yet,' Bean pointed out, 'he is a lover of truth!'

Sipping his tea with the new arrival, Murdoch, the wordy Bartlett launched into his favourite theme: his criticism of the British leadership, the British general staff and the British plans. *He saw only doom ahead.* He admitted he was not liked at HQ for his carping denigration of the British strategy on Gallipoli, but he didn't care.

Next on the Murdoch introduction list was 58-year-old Henry Nevinson, the reporter representing the British provincial press. A courtly man, serious like Bean, Nevinson was considered one of the best correspondents on Imbros, a stickler for accuracy and the rules, with a sense of duty that was to soon lead him to take an action Keith Murdoch was unlikely to thank him for ... Bean thought Nevinson a more accurate writer than Bartlett, a clever talker, 'but not with Bartlett's extraordinary sparkle'.

Next morning, with Bartlett's graphic descriptions of British bungling ringing in his ears, Murdoch took off for Anzac. He was never to forget a detail of what he saw, and he lost no time in cabling back his first impressions to Australia for publication:

> For five months they have lived on a solitary desert spot where every day brings its new test of sinew and every night its new test of courage: where no one is safe from wound and death, and no physique is proof against the physical trials. It is only a strip of shell-torn beach and cliff and gully, with deep hat-high saps leading from place to place, and all life dependent upon the protection afforded by sand bags ...
>
> I have given only a bare impression of life at Anzac ...
>
> Life that is spiritual, mental and physical pain. I have not exaggerated - far from it. No one at home can imagine what it is. It is worse than any picture conjured by inexperienced, peaceable Australians.

The men are stoical, but not contemptuous. I have been told that the soul of Anzac has completely changed, and that until the Turkish debacle of early May, when they left at least 4000 dead in front of our trenches, the spirit of the invincible First Division was one of complete defiance. Our soldiers then had the elation that knew no fear, and they defied the Turks as much as they despised them. Nothing anyone can say will detract from the glory of those great days, when men died charging with the light of battle in their eyes and stuck it out - though without water and wounded. But the visitor now thinks he sees something even finer in this dying and suffering in full knowledge of war and with full understanding of the previous deaths and long sufferings of this little shell-torn spot.

He was on the Peninsula, tramping the beaches, clambering through the trenches and climbing the dizzy slopes for four days, which was long enough. While Murdoch was questioning weary, drawn soldiers and their officers about the war, he was also making his inquiries about the mail problems, being informed that the mails were efficiently handled once they had arrived, but there were distribution problems further back along the line, particularly at Mudros. He got back to Cairo in the second week of September and immediately began probing the mail situation there. What he discovered made him so hot under the collar he shot off a hurried note to Senator George Pearce telling him the mails question 'must be urgently faced'.

The men value their letters next to their lives, and they can get few or no letters after they have left the firing line. In hospital the present mail arrangements have collapsed. The only remedy is the one I suggested to you by cable, and which I fully outline in a report I am sending you tomorrow. It means a big change in Australian methods ... but be very firm with the postal department, if you want our wounded men to hear from their homes ... Such delays are wholly inexcusable in Melbourne. When one gets into the firing line one realises how inexcusable is delay away from Melbourne. I also cabled suggesting changes in the cable system and regarding information about wounded, but no replies have come ... Three cables were sent to your department three weeks ago, each concerning an urgent matter, and they have not even been acknowledged. I had a thorough round of the Peninsula and talked a great deal with Hamilton and Bird-wood. I hope you will not think I am reflecting their views when I say that old brigadiers should not be sent. It is no place for a man over 50 years of age. Indeed, it is a place only for youth. Without doubt some of our brigadiers have cost us many lives through their ignorance and through their inadaptability to these extraordinary conditions. Monash and Hughes dashed their men against a high post here - Baby Seven Hundred - and they should have known after the first line went out that the job was hopeless. It was pitiful - fine Australian heart and soul and muscle wiped out in an impossible task.
    Oh, there is a lot of murder through incapacity. I am no defender of the British officer, especially after what I have seen here; but I do say that men like Hughes and Burston should not be sent.

But the grim-faced newspaperman in the crumpled trousers and heavy boots had far more serious things occupying his mind than letters to soldiers. He had worried

Ellis Ashmead-Bartlett, the English war correspondent who first put doubts in Murdoch's mind about what was going on at Anzac. Ashmead-Bartlett's own letter to Prime Minister Asquith was taken from Murdoch at Marseilles. (BBC Hulton Picture Library)

over taking a most solemn step in his journalistic career, and while he agonised over it he had to quickly make up his mind about agreeing to another: Ashmead-Bartlett came to him and handed him a sealed letter addressed to Asquith, the British Prime Minister. 'Will you take it to London with you?' Murdoch did not ask Bartlett what was in the letter, but having listened to his pessimistic views of Hamilton's conduct of the war, he could guess what it might contain. He nodded. Yes, he would carry it.

Murdoch went aboard ship for England, Bartlett's letter in his pocket and with turmoil in his mind: for *he* was also deciding about whether to attack Hamilton ...

When the ship arrived at Marseilles Murdoch noticed that one of the first figures up the gangplank was a British Army officer. The man sought him out and introduced himself as an intelligence officer. 'I have a wire from Lord French to ask you if you are carrying any letters.'

'Yes, I have one,' admitted Keith Murdoch. 'It is for the Prime Minister of England.'

The officer explained that he had the authority to request the letter and Murdoch handed it over. 'Will it reach the Prime Minister?' he asked. The officer said he presumed so and gave Murdoch a receipt. Then he asked to see Murdoch's other papers and rummaged through them, taking the only copy Murdoch had of his report to the Australian government about the inefficiency of the mails. He was never to see it again.

Who had sold out the courier?

Charles Bean was able to explain, years later, that Henry Nevinson had heard whispers of the Bartlett-Murdoch scheme and feeling that the honour of the correspondents had been compromised, had gone to Hamilton, who immediately sent for Ashmead-Bartlett. Was this true? demanded Hamilton. Yes, admitted the correspondent. But he refused to divulge the contents of his letter.

Hamilton found it almost impossible to contain his anger about such a betrayal. His mood was worse when the War Office cabled confirming that his fears were correct. Ashmead-Bartlett *had* written a letter for the PM and it had 'criticised military operations'. A few tents away, Charles Bean was recording the sensational camp gossip in his diary:

> Tonight two officers came back from GHQ with Bartlett. I was writing in the mess tent when they told me Bartlett was going home. 'Lucky beggar,' I said. And presently some mention came up of his return. 'Well, as a matter of fact he's not returning,' they said. 'He's got the sack.' Bartlett was in Nevinson's tent when I went into it and he told me to stay. It was true ... He had got Murdoch, the Australian *Sun* correspondent, who was going to London, to take home with him a letter to the Prime Minister putting the state of things here in a somewhat crude light. It was a brilliantly written letter, rather overstating the case as Bartlett always does, but a great deal of it was unanswerable and badly needs understanding. It made two assumptions. 1. that the Suvla-Sari Bair Plan (that of the second great effort in Gallipoli in August) could never have succeeded and could have accomplished nothing if it had succeeded - which I think is false; it was very difficult but contained a distinct chance of solid success; and 2. that a landing at Bulair would have succeeded and would still succeed - which is possible but which is by no means taken for granted.
>
> Bartlett's letter was worth the consideration of any man and I've no doubt it will be considered in time. Several members of the Cabinet asked him to write to them privately

A base scene at Suvla Bay, 'a shallow, open indentation . . . the flat country leading from the beach consists mainly of a marsh called Bitter Lake, which in winter becomes a great morass. After heavy rains the flat is inundated.' (Australian War Memorial G533)

which was not a very loyal thing for them to do. But then politicians are not loyal. He made one mistake I think: he ought to have taken the letter home himself after he had written all he had wanted to (for his newspapers) about the battles of August. It was difficult. It would have been scarcely loyal to his employers to go home and leave the work here, and I don't know if he would have been allowed to return. Unless he went, I don't think the letter could have been got through, the censors would not have passed it.

If Hamilton believed this turn of events a betrayal, there was far worse news in store for him.

Murdoch was down in his steamer cabin turning over in his mind a way to prepare his own indictment of what he believed was shocking conduct of the war and senseless waste of life at Anzac. If he went ahead he would be perpetrating a journalistic act he would never be allowed to forget for the rest of his life. He knew full well that as a reporter allowed at the Front he had signed – and was bound by – an agreement that he would send out no newspaper report that had not been passed by the censor.

Murdoch, however, did not have a newspaper report in mind. He was planning a letter to his Prime Minister. But, argued one part of his conscience, wasn't such a letter barred by the pledge he had given? After all, the piece of paper he had put his name to in front of Hamilton had said: '... and bind myself not to attempt to correspond by any other route or by any other means than that officially sanctioned.' It was that very clause which had given British Army Intelligence what they believed was the right to seize Bartlett's letter.

No – said the other part of his conscience – there was a way; an official way. It had been made clear by the War Office that soldiers disgruntled about what was happening to them, wherever they were, had a solemn right, protected by law, a right *to correspond to a minister of the crown*. And as Murdoch remembered it the War Office allowed 'any correspondent' such right.

Somewhere at sea as the ship rolled onwards towards the white cliffs of Dover, Murdoch came to his decision. He sat at his dressing-table and wrote down a rough draft of what he would tell Andrew Fisher back in Australia. (When his colleague Campbell-Jones at the United Cable Service was allowed to read this draft he said: 'I have never perused any official document more packed with scorching phrases, more brutal in its utter frankness, more instinct with earnest truth ...')

4 The Gallipoli letter

Murdoch disembarked on 21 September 1915 and made his way directly to *The Times* office. After greetings from Campbell-Jones and reading mail that was awaiting him he sat down at a typewriter and began tapping out, with his two forefingers, his savage condemnation of the military minds in charge on the Peninsula.

Two days later he had finished the 8,000-word letter and took it to be dispatched to Andrew Fisher 12,000 miles away. This (in part) is what he said:

I now write of the unfortunate Dardanelles expedition, in the light of what knowledge I could gain on the spot, on the lines of communication and in Egypt.

It is undoubtedly one of the most terrible chapters in our history. Your fears have been justified. I have not military knowledge to be able to say whether the enterprise ever had a chance of succeeding. Certainly there has been a series of disastrous underestimations, and I think our Australian generals are right when they say that had any one of these been, luckily, so unEnglish a thing as an overestimation, we should have been through to Constantinople at much less cost than we have paid for our slender perch on the cliffs of the Peninsula . . .

I visited most parts of Anzac and Suvla Bay positions, walked many miles through the trenches, conversed with the leaders and what senior and junior officers I could reach, and was favoured in all parts with full and frank confidence. I could not visit Helles where we have about 25,000 men and many animals and cars (armoured cars hidden helpless in trenches!). We have abandoned our intentions of taking Achi Baba by frontal assault. This was always a hopeless scheme, after early May, and no one can understand why Hamilton persisted with it. Achi Baba is a gradual, bare slope, a mass of trenches and gun emplacements, but so little did the General Staff know of its task that it expected to storm it with ease . . .

A strong advance inland from Anzac has never been attempted. It is broken, rough, scrubby country, full of gullies and sharp ridges, and it is all within easy range of the guns of the Turkish forts at the Narrows, and their artillery on Achi Baba and round about. No serious advance could be made direct inland from this quarter. Our men I found immensely proud of their little progress on the plateau on our right - Lone Pine Plateau. Walker and Whyte thought it brilliant and wonderfully successful. But I found that we had paid 2500 men for this advance, on a short front of 300 yards! That is the only sort of advance we can make from Anzac proper.

Suvla Bay is a shallow, open indentation in the thickest part of the peninsula, about two miles and a half to the left of Anzac. The flat country leading from the beach consists mostly of a marsh called Bitter Lake, which in winter becomes a great morass. After heavy rains the flat is inundated.

On this flat in August nearly 90,000 men were landed. They were New Army and

A trench at Lone Pine. Murdoch discovered that 2500 men were killed attempting an advance on a front of 300 yards. (Australian War Memorial A2025)

Territorial divisions. They had spent a fortnight on the water, in transports which even the most careful arrangements could not make wholesome. I was on the lower deck on one of these, and the place was putrid. The men could not be allowed on shore at ports of call.

You can imagine, then that these fresh, raw, untried troops under amateur officers, homesick and apprehensive, were under normal in morale when the day of landing approached. They had to be packed like sardines on the trawlers and small destroyers and vessels for the actual landing, and were kept like this for most of an afternoon and the whole of a night. Before this embarkation, they had each received three days' supply of iron rations - biscuits and bully beef - and had filled their water bottles - one bottle to each man.

Then in the early hours came the landing, when the life of man is at its lowest.

I do not say that better arrangements could have been made. But I do say that in the first place to send raw, young recruits on this perilous enterprise was to court disaster; and Hamilton would have some reasonableness behind his complaints that his men let him down, if he and his staff had not at the same time let the men down with greater wrong-doings.

The landing was unopposed; the Turks were taken completely by surprise. But with great celerity they galloped their artillery round, and opened fire also from their forts. Before the new troops had advanced any distance they were being racked with shell fire.

I am informed by many officers that one division went ashore without any orders whatsoever. Another division to which had been allotted the essential work of occupying the Anafarta Hills were marched far to the left before the mistake in direction was noticed. It was then recalled and reformed, and sent off towards the ridge. As a practical man how much water do you think would be left in these thirsty English boys' bottles by this time - after the night on the seas, and the hot march out, march back, and advance? Of course, not a drop.

I am of course only repeating what I have been told on all hands. But you will trust me when I say that the work of the general staff in Gallipoli has been deplorable.

The 9th Army Corps reached Anafarta Hills, but could not maintain their position. Of the terrible manner of their retreat I need not tell you in this letter. One of our generals, who had his men trying desperately to hold onto the shoulders of 971 and Chunuk Bair (only a few Ghurkas reached 971 and a few Australasians Chunuk Bair), was staggered to see the 9th and 10th Corps retreats, at the very time when their firm holding was essential. He was staggered by its manner, and principally by the obvious conflicts and confusions between British Generals, due I am told to the disinclination of two of them to accept orders from De Lisle, who though junior had been placed in command after the recall of General Stopford. At least two generals were recalled at once.

Perhaps this awful defeat of August 6-10, in which our Imperial armies lost 35 per cent of their strength - 33,000 men - was due as much to inferior troops as to any other cause. But that cannot be said of the desperate effort made on August 21, after the Turks had had plenty of time in which to bring up strong reinforcements and to increase the natural strength of their positions, to take their positions by frontal assault. Some of the finest forces on the Peninsula were used in this bloody battle ...

They and other troops were dashed against the Turkish lines and broken. They never had a chance of holding their positions when for one brief hour they pierced the Turks' first line: and the slaughter of fine youth was appalling. My criticism is that, as these troops were available, they should undoubtedly have been used in early August; and to fling them, without even the element of surprise, against such trenches as the Turks make, was murder ...

We have to face ... the frightful weakening effect of sickness. Already the flies are spreading dysentery to an alarming extent, and the sick rate would astonish you. It cannot be less than 600 a day. We must be evacuating fully 1000 sick and wounded men every day. When the autumn rains come and unbury our dead, now lying under a light soil in our trenches, sickness must increase. Even now the stench in many of our trenches is sickening. Alas, the good human stuff that there lies buried, the brave hearts still, the sorrow in our hard-hit Australian households.

Supposing we lose only 30,000 during winter from sickness. That means that when spring comes we shall have about 60,000 men left. But they will not be an army. They will be a broken force, spent. A winter in Gallipoli will be a winter under severe strain, under shell fire, under the expectation of attack, and in the anguish which is inescapable on this shell-torn spot. The troops will in reality be on guard throughout the winter. They will stand to arms throughout long and bitter nights. Nothing can be expected from them when at last the normal fighting days come again. The new offensive must then be made with a huge army of new troops. Can we get them? Already the complaint in France is that we cannot fill the gaps, that after an advance our thinned ranks cannot be replenished.

But I am not a pessimist, and if there is really military necessity for this awful ordeal, then I am sure the Australian troops will face it. Indeed, anxious though they are to leave the dreary and sombre scene of their wreckage, the Australian divisions would strongly resent the confession of failure that a withdrawal would entail. They are dispirited, they

British troops sheltering on Cape Helles. 'You would refuse to believe that these men were really British soldiers . . . they show an atrophy of mind and body that is appalling.' (Australian War Memorial G330)

have been through such warfare as no army has seen in any part of the world, but they are game to the end.

On the high political question of whether good is to be served by keeping the armies in Gallipoli, I can say little, for I am uninformed. Cabinet ministers here impress me with the fact that a failure in the Dardanelles would have most serious results in India. Persia is giving endless trouble, and there seems to be little doubt that India is ripe for trouble. Nor do I know whether the appalling outlay in money on the Dardanelles expedition, with its huge and costly line of communications, can be allowed to continue without endangering those financial resources on which we rely to so great an extent in the wearing down of Germany's strength . . .

You would have wept with Hughes, and myself, if you had gone with us over the ground where two of our finest Light Horse regiments were wiped out in ten minutes in a brave effort to advance a few yards to Dead Man's Ridge. We lost five hundred men, squatters' sons and farmers' sons, on that terrible spot. Such is the cost of so much as looking out over the top of our trenches.

And now one word about the troops. No one who sees them at work in trenches and on beaches and in saps can doubt that their morale is very severely shaken indeed. It is far worse at Suvla, although the men there are only two months from home, than anywhere else. The spirit at Suvla is simply deplorable. The men have no confidence in the staff, and to tell the truth they have little confidence in London. I shall always remember the stricken face of a young English lieutenant when I told him he must make up his mind for a winter campaign. He had had a month of physical and mental torture, and the prospect of a winter seemed more than he could bear. But his greatest dread was that the London authorities would not begin until too late to send winter provisions. All the new army is still clothed in tropical uniforms, and when I left, London was still sending out drafts in thin 'shorts'. Everywhere one encountered the same fear that the armies would be left to their fate, and that the many shipments of materials, food and clothing required for winter would not be despatched until the weather made their landing impossible. This lack of confidence in the authorities arises principally from the fact that every man knows that the last operations were grossly bungled by the general staff, and that Hamilton has led a series of armies into a series of cul-de-sacs. You would hardly believe the evidence of your own eyes at Suvla. You would refuse to believe that these men were really British soldiers. So badly shaken are they by their miserable defeats and by their surroundings, so physically affected are they by the lack of water and the monotony of salt beef and rice diet, that they show an atrophy of mind and body that is appalling. I must confess that in our own trenches, where our men have been kept on guard for abnormally long periods, I saw the same terrible atrophy. You can understand how it arises. It is like the look of a tortured dumb animal. Men living in trenches with no movement except when they are digging, and with nothing to look at except a narrow strip of sky and the blank walls of their prisons, cannot remain cheerful or even thoughtful. Perhaps some efforts could have been made by the War Office to provide them with cinemas, or entertainments, but of course Gallipoli is at the end of a long and costly, not to say dangerous, line of communications.

The physique of those at Suvla is not to be compared with that of the Australians. Nor is their intelligence. I fear also that the British physique is much below that of the Turks. Indeed, it is quite obviously so. Our men have found it impossible to form a high opinion of the British K men and territorials. They are merely a lot of childlike youths without strength to endure or brains to improve their conditions. I do not like to dictate this sentence, even for your eyes, but the fact is that after the first day at Suvla an order had to be issued to officers to shoot without mercy any soldiers who lagged behind or loitered in an advance ...

At Anzac the morale is good. The men are thoroughly dispirited, except the new arrivals. They are weakened badly by dysentery and illness. They have been overworked, through lack of reinforcements. And as an army of offence they are done. Not one step can be made with the First Australian division until it has been completely rested and refitted ...

But I could pour into your ears so much truth about the grandeur of our Australian army, and the wonderful affection of these fine young soldiers for each other and their homeland, that your Australianism would become a more powerful sentiment than before. It is stirring to see them, magnificent manhood, swinging their fine limbs as they walk about Anzac. They have the noble faces of men who have endured. Oh, if you could picture Anzac as I have seen it, you would find that to be an Australian is the greatest privilege the world has to offer.

But for the general staff, and I fear for Hamilton, officers and men have nothing but contempt. They express it fearlessly. That however is not peculiar to Anzac. Sedition is talked round every tin of bully beef on the peninsula, and it is only loyalty that holds the forces together. Every returning troopship, every section of the line of communications, is full of the same talk. I like General Hamilton and found him exceedingly kindly. I admire him as a journalist. But as a strategist he has completely failed. Undoubtedly, the essential and first step to restore the morale of the shaken forces is to recall him and

Camp at Imbros Island. Troops left here on 6 August 1915 for the ill-fated landing at Suvla Bay. (Australian War Memorial G676)

his Chief of Staff, a man more cordially detested in our forces than Enver Pasha. What the army here wants is a young leader, a man who has had no past, and around whom the officers can rally . . .

I cannot see any solution which does not begin with the recall of Hamilton . . .

It is not for me to judge Hamilton, but it is plain that when an army has completely lost faith in its general, and he has on numerous occasions proved his weaknesses, only one thing can be done. He has very seldom been at Anzac. He lives at Imbros. The French call him the General who lives on an Island. The story may not be true, but the army believes that Hamilton left Suvla on August 21 remarking 'Everything hangs in the balance, the Yeomanry are about to charge'. Of course the army laughs at a general who leaves the battlefield when everything hangs in the balance.

What I want to say to you now very seriously is that the continuous and ghastly bungling over the Dardanelles enterprise was to be expected from such a General Staff as the British Army possesses, so far as I have seen it. The conceit and complacency of the red feather men are equalled only by their incapacity. Along the lines of communi-

cations, and especially at Mudros, are countless high officers and conceited young cubs who are plainly only playing at war. What can you expect of men who have never worked seriously, who have lived for their appearance and for social distinction and self satisfaction, and who are now called on to conduct a gigantic war? Kitchener has a terrible task in getting pure work out of these men, whose motives can never be pure, for they are unchangeably selfish. I want to say frankly that it is my opinion, and that without exception of Australian officers, that appointments to the General Staff are made from motives of friendship and special influence. Australians now loathe and detest any Englishman wearing red ... I could tell you of many scandals, but the instance that will best appeal to you is that of the staff ship Aragon. She is a magnificent and luxurious South American liner, anchored in Mudros harbour as a base for the Inspector-General of Communications. I can give you no idea of how the Australians - and the new British officers too - loathe the Aragon. Heaven knows what she is costing, but certainly the staff lives in luxury. And nothing can exceed the rudeness of these chocolate general staff soldiers to those returning from the Front. The ship's adjutant is the worst instance of rude and disgusting snobbishness and incapacity I have come across. With others, plain downright incapacity is the main characteristic. I must say this of them also, that whereas at our 3rd Australian General Hospital on shore we had 134 fever cases, including typhus, with only a few mosquito nets, and *no ice*, and few medical comforts, the Aragon staff was wallowing in ice. Colonel Stawell - you know him as Melbourne's leading consultant - and Sir Alex McCormick are not sentimentalists. But they really wept over the terrible hardships of the wounded, due to the incapacity of the Aragon. One concrete case is that of 150 wounded men landed in dead of night, with no provisions and no instructions, at the hospital beach, to make their way as best they could to the hospital, which had no notice of their arrival. While I was at the hospital a beautiful general and his staff rode in to make an inspection. Despite their appearance as perfect specimens of the general staff, I thought we shall now get the ice from the Aragon on to the brows of our unfortunate men. But no ice appeared next day.

You will think that all this is a sorry picture, but do not forget that the enemy has his troubles, and that we have certain signs that his morale is deteriorating. From what I saw of the Turk I am convinced that he is a brave and generous foe, and he is fighting now for dear home, with a feeling that he is winning, and that he is a better man than

Office of the Commandant of the advanced base at Suvla Bay. Murdoch revealed that General Sir Ian Hamilton had seldom been at Anzac, or even near the front of a battle. (Australian War Memorial G436)

those opposed to him. The Turks by the way are as generous in their praise of our men as the British and French are. Certainly the Turks are positively afraid of our men, and one of their trenches - that opposite Quinn's Post - is such a place of fear, owing to the indomitable way in which our snipers and bomb-throwers have got their men down, that Turks will not go into it unless they are made corporals.

I hope I have not made the picture too gloomy. I have great faith still in the Englishman ... But this unfortunate expedition has never been given a chance. It required large bodies of seasoned troops. It required a great leader. It required self-sacrifice on the part of the staff as well as that sacrifice so wonderfully and liberally made on the part of the soldiers. It has had none of these things. Its troops have been second class, because (they were) untried before their awful battles and privations of the peninsula. And behind it all is the gross selfishness and complacency on the part of the staff.

Much more I could tell you, but my task is done ... This of course is a private letter, but you will show it to George Pearce and Hughes, so I shall say nothing more than the plain goodbye of a friend.
Sincerely yours,
Keith Murdoch

Murdoch interrupted his typing shortly after midday on 22 September to set off for lunch at Simpsons in the Strand with Campbell-Jones and *The Times* editor, Geoffrey Dawson. While waiters were busy carving the beef at mobile trolleys, Murdoch told the two men, at first hand, what it was like at Gallipoli. 'Dawson was at once moved by the sincerity and the vividness of his word-pictures,' said Campbell-Jones afterwards.

Geoffrey Dawson, editor of The Times, *who first persuaded Murdoch to speak to the British cabinet on the Dardanelles situation. He was to remain a close and influential friend. (BBC Hulton Picture Library)*

The trio returned to Printing House Square and Murdoch got on with the two-finger job of pecking out his letter on his battered little Hermes. The phone in Campbell-Jones's office rang and it was Dawson, still shaken by what he had been told. Could Murdoch be persuaded to repeat what he had said to a member of the British cabinet? Sir Edward Carson, chairman of the cabinet's Dardanelles Committee, for instance? Murdoch said he would, and it was arranged that he would take breakfast the next morning with Carson.

Murdoch went through his harrowing story again. After he had left, Carson lost no time in repeating to the war cabinet what the journalist had told him. Lloyd George, at the time Minister for Munitions, listened with rapt attention. The members had before them the 'red tabs' reports filed from Sir Ian Hamilton's headquarters, and these gave the impression that victory was only weeks, or at the worst, months away. Some members shook their heads; Murdoch's outpourings could only be exaggerated, sensational journalism.

On 25 September, two days after sending his letter off to Australia, Murdoch was persuaded by Lloyd George and Lord Murray of Elibank, to let the British Prime Minister, Asquith, see a copy. Reluctantly he agreed to do so, and sent it off with the accompanying note:

Arundel Hotel, Victoria Embankment
September 25, 1915
The Right Honorable H.H. Asquith, P.C., M.P., Prime Minister.
Dear Sir,
Mr Lloyd George has suggested to me that I should place at your disposal whatever knowledge I gained of the Dardanelles operations while an Australian civilian representative there.

I therefore take the liberty of sending to you a copy of a private letter I have addressed to Mr Fisher, in conformance with his request that I should write him fully on the subject.

This letter was, of course, intended only for Commonwealth Ministers, and contains references which will have no interest to you. But I feel justified in sending it to you, because if it adds one iota to your information, or presents the Australian point of view, it will be of service in this most critical moment.

I write with diffidence, and only at Mr Lloyd George's request. In any case, you will know that my motive is one of affectionate regard for our soldiers' interests.
I have the honour to be,
Your obedient servant,
Keith Murdoch

Anti-Dardanelles feeling among British ministers was stirring. Many were alarmed at the lack of information coming from Hamilton. Now, as they read through Murdoch's pages of accusations, they had the ammunition they wanted. Asquith was persuaded that the letter was so vital that it should be printed and circulated as a State paper. Murdoch now found himself in the awesome position of being interviewed, cross-examined and lunched by such figures as Bonar Law, the Conservative Party Leader, Lord Kitchener, Secretary for War, Edward Grey, the Foreign Secretary, and Winston Churchill, First Lord of the Admiralty (no friend of the anti-Dardanelles group), who called the letter 'lurid'. While the interviews went on, Murdoch's words were being printed on the duck-egg blue stationery of the Committee of Imperial Defence and distributed to the cabinet as a confidential document. The snowball was now gathering momentum. To add to its impetus, Ashmead-Bartlett arrived in London fresh from his dismissal from Imbros and hurried off to meet Lord Northcliffe, proprietor of *The Times* and the *Daily Mail*, quickly convincing this powerful figure that the Dardanelles should be evacuated.

It was now turning bitterly cold on Imbros and preparations were being made to shift GHQ to the westerly, more sheltered side of the island. A stone shack, rather like a shepherd's hut, had been prepared for Hamilton, though he was still in his tent when a dispatch box arrived on 13 October with a copy of the Murdoch letter. Attached to it was a note from General Calwell, director of Military Operations, who said he was doubtful whether to send it on at all ... 'this man has listened to every bit of tittle-tattle that he heard whilst in Egypt and the Dardanelles and has written it down as solid fact for communication to his Prime Minister'. Hamilton read through what Murdoch had written and felt it, he said later, 'like a hit below the belt'.

He had been pestered by the Dardanelles Committee (now in effect the War Council) for his estimates of losses, should evacuation be ordered. The Committee realised it faced an agonising decision on the conduct of the war: to renew the French offensive; to concentrate on Salonika; to support Gallipoli or get out. Kitchener's last cable to Hamilton asked for his estimate of losses if evacuation was decided upon. He replied that evacuation was 'unthinkable', but if it was ordered, he would lose 35-40 per cent of his men. His general staff's estimate was even gloomier - 50 per cent at least.

Winter time at Anzac. Murdoch said that Gallipoli troops would not survive another winter on the Peninsula. His 'Gallipoli letter' prompted a successful gradual, secret withdrawal of the troops. (Australian War Memorial A769)

Hamilton sat up that night replying to Murdoch's letter and his repudiation was cabled off the next day:

I have read Mr Murdoch's letter with care, and I have tried to give it my most impartial consideration and not to allow myself in reply to be influenced in any way by the criticisms he may have felt himself bound to make upon myself personally. What does this letter amount to? Here we have a man, a journalist by profession, one who is quick to seize every point, and to coin epithets, which throws each fleeting impression into strongest relief. He comes armed with a natural and justifiable enthusiastic admiration for everything connected with the Commonwealth to which he belongs, and ready to retail to his Minister or his public anything that can contribute to show the troops they have sent in an heroic light.

Here he obtains his first sight of war and of the horrors and hardships inseparable from it. He finds men who have just been through some of the hardest fighting imaginable and who have suffered terrible losses; he finds probably that very many of those whom he hoped to see, certainly many of those of whose welfare their motherland would wish to hear, are killed, wounded or laid up with illness - he finds all this and he becomes very deeply depressed. In such an atmosphere Mr Murdoch composes his letter, a general analysis of which shows it to be divided, to my mind, into two separate strata.

First, an appreciation in burning terms of the spirit, the achievements, and all soldierly qualities of the Australian forces. Secondly, a condemnation, as sweeping and as unrelieved as his praise in the first instance is unstinted, of the whole of the rest of the force.

I myself as Commander-in-Chief, my generals, my staff, lines of communication, Sir John Maxwell and General Spens at the Base, even the British soldier collectively and individually, are all embraced in this condemnation which is completed by the inclusion of the entire direction of the forces at home, both naval and military.

Where all are thus tarred with the same brush I am content to leave it to the impartial reader to decide what reliance can be placed on Mr Murdoch's judgment. My own feeling certainly is that, in his admiration for the Australian forces, and in his grief at their heavy losses (in both of which feelings I fully share), he has allowed himself to belittle and to criticise us all so that their virtues might be thrown into even bolder relief.

With Mr Murdoch's detailed points I do not propose to deal, nor do I think you expect me to do so. On every page inaccuracies of fact abound. The breaking of Spens on the Continent, a theatre of war he has never visited; the over- statement of our casualties by more than 40 per cent; the acceptance as genuine of a wholly mythical order about the shooting of laggards - really the task would be too long. As to the value of Mr Murdoch's appreciation of the strategical and tactical elements of the situation you can yourself assess them at their true value.

Finally, I do not for one moment believe the general statement put forward to the effect that the troops are disheartened. Neither the statement nor the assertion that they are discontented with the British officers commanding them has the slightest foundation in fact.

A postscript read:

I attach correspondence showing how Mr Murdoch's visit arose. I believe I exceeded my power in giving him permission to come, but I was most anxious to oblige the Australian Prime Minister and Senator Pearce. You will see that he promises faithfully to observe any conditions I may impose. The only condition I imposed was that he should sign a declaration identical with that which I attach. He signed and the paper is in my possession.

'Anzac Cove' by F. Crozier – a view of the cove as it looked when Keith Murdoch first arrived in August 1915 to investigate complaints about the postal facilities in the Middle East. (Australian War Memorial 43)

A side view of Cruden Farm, 30 miles from Melbourne, which was bought by Keith Murdoch in the mid-1920s. Below: the stable yard at Cruden Farm – the Murdochs had a large number of horses and ponies.

General Sir Ian Hamilton and his chief of staff, General Braithwaite, 'a man more cordially detested . . . than Enver Pasha', being rowed to their headquarters on Imbros Island. (Australian War Memorial G328)

Hamilton was due to move from his tent the following day, and had just retired for the night when an officer arrived with a message, marked 'Secret and Personal'. It was from the War Secretary, Lord Kitchener. 'When the next message arrives,' it instructed him, 'you should decipher it yourself.' Should he awaken the general when the cable arrived, inquired the officer? No, Hamilton said. It should be brought at the usual hour the next morning.

Hamilton had ready the cipher book (and a device like a bow-string which had to be used in conjunction) to decode the message when it was handed to him. Alone in his tent he spelled out each word:

> The War Council held last night decided that though the Government fully appreciate your work and the gallant manner in which you personally have struggled to make the enterprise a success in face of the terrible difficulties you have had to contend against, they, all the same, wish to make a change in the command which will give them an opportunity of seeing you.

His chief of staff, Braithwaite, was to go as well. General Sir Charles Monro, one of the Army commanders on the Western Front, would be sent to replace Hamilton. Hamilton - stunned - said his farewells. There was an emotional dinner for him aboard the *Triad* and on 17 October he and Braithwaite went aboard the cruiser *Chatham*. They watched Imbros gradually fade from view and went below, only to be called again to the quarter-deck. Hamilton found the *Chatham* steering a corkscrew course between the anchored ships of the Fleet, and sailors lining the decks of each one, cheering him on his way...

While nothing of his sensational letter had been published in the Fleet-st. papers, Murdoch was cabling his Australian newspapers a week before Hamilton's recall:

> The necessity for looking the Dardanelles position squarely in the face has been forced upon the Cabinet and I am sure that within the next few days a policy will be adopted which will be firm and fearless and will perhaps for the first time prove that the tremendous nature of the task is understood.

He was in a position - an *inside* position - to know.

Monro stepped on to Imbros and a cable from Kitchener was handed to him almost before he had had time to unpack. It said: 'Please send me as soon as possible your report on the main issue, namely, leaving or staying.' Within six hours the methodical, 55-year-old Monro had visited each of the bridgeheads and assessed the situation, which was, to say the least, depressing. He cabled Kitchener next day recommending evacuation of the Peninsula. His estimate of probable losses: 40,000 men. Kitchener was appalled. He said he would never sign an evacuation order. Then Commodore Roger Keyes, who had tried once before, came to him with a bold plan: a headlong naval assault on the Narrows with a simultaneous bombardment of the Turkish shore batteries, cutting the single road supplying the twenty Turkish divisions now stationed on the Peninsula.

While the evacuation-naval attack idea was being argued in London the worst blizzard the Dardanelles had seen for forty years swept down over the trenches, cliffs and beaches. Nevinson wrote of the men staggering about in the storm: 'They could neither hear nor speak, but stared about them like bewildered bullocks.' Rain and violent thunderstorms, followed by snow and sleet, left sentries early in the morning dead but still standing, clutching rifles that had fused to their hands. Two hundred soldiers were drowned and five thousand suffered frostbite.

Then, three weeks of absolutely calm weather enabled dug-outs to be roofed, new blankets, boots and oil-stoves to be landed. While soldiers talked about sitting through a terrible winter yet another plan was being discussed: *a gradual, secret withdrawal.* It

Australian graves at Gallipoli: '. . . the slaughter of fine youth was appalling.' Five hundred men were wiped out in ten minutes in a brave attempt to advance a few yards. (Australian War Memorial G419)

would take place on successive nights, leaving a small holding garrison to man the trenches to the last and to make their escape on the final rescue craft. It was agreed after deep and often bitter argument. The signal was given, and at dusk each evening, flotillas of small craft set off and crept into the shore and men, with boots wrapped in sacking, stepped carefully along blanket-covered jetties and on to the boats. In the first week 40,000 men had been taken off the Peninsula under the noses of the unsuspecting Turks. Two nights later the other 40,000 were evacuated without a single loss of life. There were still 35,000 men on Cape Helles. And again a withdrawal at night went into operation. When the garrison was down to 19,000, the Turks opened the heaviest artillery barrage of the campaign and it went on for four-and-a-half hours.

It calmed only for the expected infantry assault; and when that came, the British, pinned down in the trenches, answered with a steady, murderous fire which halted the attackers in their tracks.

It amazed the British to see the Turks suddenly halt. Officers lashed hysterically at soldiers and swore at them, urging them on; but they refused. And by nightfall no British line had been penetrated. The German Commander, von Sanders, was then convinced that the British had no plans to evacuate. But, at dusk, the rescue boats and warships set out once more; it was to be the last time they would head for the Peninsula. By a quarter to four in the morning every man was off the beach and safely aboard a boat. The Peninsula had been evacuated.

Correspondent Charles Bean put the officers' view of Murdoch's Gallipoli letter in a note from Anzac HQ in France in 1916: 'It is a bit of a shock for a man who lives for his profession to find out that what the whole system ... cannot do after months of close attention to the subject, a single visitor outside the profession after a few days' inspection can do; and that is, make up the mind of the British government.' (Remarkably, viewed from the modern experience of the media, Fleet-st. newspapers still kept quiet about the Murdoch letter, though it was known inside the offices that he had written a most critical account of what he had seen.)

17 October 1915: General Sir Ian Hamilton (second from right) and General Braithwaite (right) on board the Triad *after being recalled to England to answer Murdoch's allegations. Commodore Keyes (left) and Vice-Admiral de Roebuck bid them farewell. (Australian War Memorial G541)*

46

Now Murdoch was to face a most sobering, stringent cross-examination to explain what he had done.

In June 1916, Bonar Law, the Colonial Secretary, had rashly promised to lay 'the Dardanelles papers' before Parliament. There was such a horrified outcry from the War Department that his coalition colleague, Asquith, offered instead a secret Royal Commission on what had gone wrong in the Dardanelles, with a published report at the end. Andrew Fisher, now Australia's High Commissioner in London, was to sit on the Commission which over the next twelve months heard more than two hundred witnesses, including Churchill, Hamilton, Monro - and the 30-year-old Murdoch. The Commission already had before it Hamilton's hard-hitting, point-by-point denial of the veracity of what the Australian journalist had written. It was as long as Murdoch's letter itself, and in it Hamilton again refuted Murdoch's allegations that there were deaths from thirst; that the physique of British soldiers at Suvla was 'below that of the Turks', or their nature 'childlike'. Then he came to the serious allegation that orders had to be issued to shoot without mercy any soldier who lagged behind or loitered in an advance. 'Quite plainly,' said Hamilton, 'this is a shameful lie.'

(Charles Bean's diary for 26 September 1915 said specifically that Australians in some instances had to be driven ahead by the threat of being shot from behind by their officers. He went on: 'As a matter of fact anyone who has seen a battle knows that soldiers do very often run away; soldiers, even Australian soldiers, have sometimes to be threatened with a revolver to make them go on - in individual cases. I have seen it happen once to an Australian NCO whom Colonel McCay ... threatened to shoot ... and I know that others have done the same. The Turks have (sometimes) to be threatened with machine-guns from behind ...')

On the criticisms Murdoch had made against the General Staff, viz. 'conceit and self-complacency', 'equalled only by their incapacity', 'unchangeably selfish', 'chocolate general staff', Hamilton fired back: 'Could anything be more cruelly ungenerous or unjust? I will sum up these slanders ... No gentleman would have said it, and no gentleman will believe it.'

He added: 'I, a British General and a member of the Committee of Imperial Defence, have had circulated amongst my brother members aspersions against my honour, and libels against my troops. No chance was vouchsafed me of proving the malignancy of these attacks, or of showing how far they might be inspired by personal animus ... they had already been elevated to the rank of State papers, and passed round from hand to hand, and mouth to ear through the most influential circles in the land. Things being so, I must respectfully request that these remarks of mine may also be printed and may be shown (as far as possible) to all who have read the vilification of British Generals, staff, and regiments penned to his Prime Minister by Mr K.A. Murdoch.'

Murdoch saw what Hamilton had written and countered with a hurriedly typed, supplementary statement which he asked the Royal Commission to accept. In this he asked the rhetorical question regarding his decision to write the letter: 'Had I then any choice of action? Obviously I had to do my utmost to secure attention of those most powerful to gain full and immediate consideration for the expedition ... I took the action most calculated to gain ... not evacuation of our positions, but full and immediate political and military consideration. It required a fresh mind on the spot, which meant opposing General Hamilton in the strongest possible way.

'The vindictive tone of (General Hamilton's) memorandum may be partly explained by the fact that ... on arriving in London (he) found that he owed his recall to these disclosures.' The troops' opinions of General Hamilton were, he said, too painful to elaborate.

It was now time for Murdoch to stand before the Commission, be sworn, and in the cold light of day defend what he had said. It was Monday, 5 February 1917, and he had been given only three days' notice of his summons as a witness. On the forty-third day of the sittings he took his place before the Commissioners. Sir William Pickford took him over his arrival at the Dardanelles and for a few minutes the two tussled over whether or not it was proper for Murdoch to reveal the names of officers he had gathered opinions from. Then, discussing Murdoch's couriership of Ashmead-Bartlett's letter, Sir William wanted to know:

> 'I am asking you, were you not responsible for taking for him a letter which had not passed the Censor, and had never been submitted to him?'
> Murdoch: It was addressed to the Prime Minister of the United Kingdom. It was a sealed letter and marked 'Personal'. I think the position was such that I was absolutely justified. I did it in a perfectly open way. When I was asked whether I was carrying it, I said at once that I was. Which of those clauses in the Declaration (do) you think it contravenes?
> Sir William: You knew that no communications were to be sent by any correspondents except after they had passed the Censor?
> A: I question that. I think the War Office agrees that a correspondent has a right to address a Minister of the Crown.
> Q: I never heard of it.
> A: I am informed that it is so.
> Mr Walter Roch, MP (one of the Commissioners): It has been stated that anybody can correspond uncensored with a member of Parliament direct. Orders were given to troops that this was so.

Mr Andrew Fisher then asked Murdoch if he was Australian-born, to which he replied that he was. 'And you naturally felt that you would like to do the best not only for your own particular native country but the Empire's forces now and always?'

> Murdoch: I think I risked my whole career. I am always prepared to offer everything I have to Australia.

In its final judgment, the Royal Commission found that when military expedition was decided upon, sufficient consideration was not given to the measures necessary to carry it out with success. The difficulties of the operations were 'much underestimated'. At the outset all decisions were taken and all provisions based on the assumption that if a landing were effected the resistance would be slight and the advance rapid. The Commission saw no sufficient ground for such an assumption. It said: 'We are of the opinion that with the resources then available success in the Dardanelles if possible was only possible upon condition that the government concentrated their efforts upon the enterprise and limited their expenditure of men and material in the western theatre of war. This condition was never fulfilled.'

The Commission said of Sir Ian Hamilton: 'It is inevitable that the capabilities of a commander in war should be judged by the results he achieves even though, if these results are disappointing, his failure may be due to causes for which he is only partially responsible.' He had succeeded in landing his troops in April at the places he had chosen:

'but the operations that were intended immediately to follow the landing were abruptly checked owing to a miscalculation of the strength of the Turkish defences and the fighting qualities of the Turkish troops. This rebuff should have convinced Sir Ian Hamilton that the Turkish entrenchments were skilfully disposed and well armed, and that naval gun fire was ineffective against trenches and entanglements of the modern type. We doubt however whether the failure of these operations sufficiently impressed Sir Ian Hamilton and the military authorities at home with the serious nature of the opposition likely to be encountered.' The results of severe fighting that took place in June and July 'were not commensurate with the efforts made and the losses incurred.'

Hamilton was confident that the combined operations of August would be successful, but, the Commission said, 'he was again baffled by the obstinacy of the Turkish resistance. Moreover the failure of night advances in a difficult and unexplored country which formed parts of the plan led to heavy casualties and temporarily disorganised the forces employed.'

The Commission recognised Hamilton's personal gallantry and energy, his sanguine disposition and his determination to win at all costs; also that his task 'was one of extreme difficulty, the more so as the authorities at home at first misconceived the nature and duration of the operations and afterwards were slow to realise that to drive the Turks out of their entrenchments and occupy the heights commanding the Straits was a formidable and hazardous enterprise which demanded concentration of force and effort.'

5 Mr Hughes' 'fixer'

Keith Murdoch was to stay on for six years as editor and manager for the United Cable Service. During this time his stature as a journalist and 'unofficial ambassador' steadily rose.

His Gallipoli letter had already given him a friendly and lasting *entrée* to British cabinet ministers. They not only readily agreed to be interviewed by him, but gladly accepted his hospitality at his bachelor-flat dinner table. His friendship with the fiery Billy Hughes firmed. Hughes had replaced Fisher as Prime Minister and the weary Fisher had gladly accepted the sinecure in London of Australian High Commissioner. Hughes, though, saw the office as being ill-equipped to project Australia's image in Britain and turned to Murdoch, not only to have Australia's voice heard in Fleet-st., but as his personal publicist, guide-to-the-British-mind, fixer, speech editor and errand boy. When Hughes sailed to Britain in 1916 Murdoch hosted a dinner for the little Welshman in his flat. Around the table sat Hughes, General William Robertson, Chief of the Imperial General Staff, Lloyd George, Bonar Law, Lord Milner, Lord Northcliffe, the newspaper proprietor, and Geoffrey Dawson, editor of *The Times*. Hughes was capturing the political imagination of Britain, and people in high places jostled for his attention; when they couldn't easily get it, they jostled Murdoch to arrange it.

When he got home, all Hughes' toughest and most abrasive characteristics came to the fore as he quickly went into battle to achieve conscription. He enlisted Murdoch's aid to persuade the diggers at the Front to vote 'Yes' and Murdoch obediently hurried off to France. But the British Commander-in-Chief, Douglas Haig, turned down the idea of soldiers being addressed by soldiers on the question. 'It was only by fighting his whole staff,' Murdoch reported back to Hughes, 'that I got him to agree to any meetings.' And these had to be addressed by civilians. At the Front Hughes lost his conscription call; the Australian soldier was not prepared to embroil any more of his countrymen in terrible battles. Murdoch saw other reasons like a backlash against discipline and authority; the diggers wanted no conscripts among them; they were not yet a victorious army; they did not like the British and felt a great many more British should be fighting; they were influenced by the fact that the Political Labour League had come out against conscription; and they objected to 'and were bitter about' only sons being exempted. Murdoch said: 'It is a tragedy that our fine army should vote

This cartoon, which appeared in Punch *after the war, captured one aspect of the public side of Billy Hughes. (La Trobe collection, State Library of Victoria)*

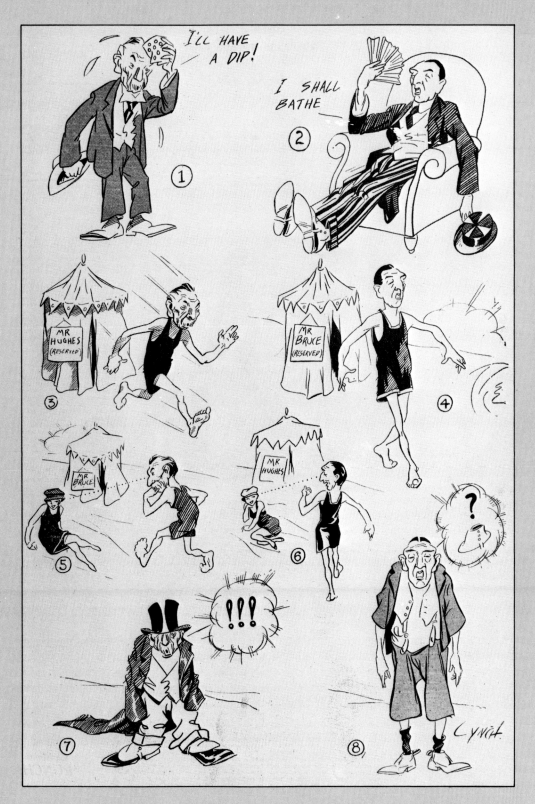

against their own reinforcements. Don't make any mistake about the feeling ... they are utterly sick of it and would welcome peace.' The count showed that Hughes had also lost at home.

When in the early months of 1917 volunteers were not coming forward at a sufficient rate to keep the five AIF divisions up to effective strength, demand grew for a second conscription call. Again the referendum was lost - by an even larger majority than in 1916. But this time the troops outside Australia voted 'Yes', 91,365; 'No' 89,743. The overall majority for 'No' was 166,588.

Keith Murdoch with Billy Hughes in France in 1918. Hughes used Murdoch as his personal publicist, 'fixer', speech editor and errand boy. Years later, the relationship would turn sour. (Australian War Memorial E2650)

By now Hughes had Murdoch working hard for him, shuttling between Whitehall ministries, buttonholing officials and politicians. And as he met more and more of the great, Murdoch himself was becoming a little like the irascible little man who pulled the strings: *he* too started interfering. It was not enough to cable back his opinions to be printed in the various Australian newspapers (a reporter's transgression that Campbell-Jones sarcastically criticised: 'It is not the personal views of Keith Murdoch which we and our clients are buying') - by September 1917 Murdoch had started to urge Haig at British GHQ in France to listen to the Australian Government's desire for the formation of a single army corps under the command of Australian officers. Haig said it was impracticable and unwieldy. Murdoch wrote next day to General Sir Lancelot Kiggell, Haig's chief of staff, who had been present when he saw Haig:

> When Sir Douglas and yourself mentioned yesterday the possibility of certain changes in the Australian Corps staffs, I fear I became absorbed in telling you of the great regard

we have for the ability and character of our Australian soldier, White, and I did not grasp the full significance of the remarks until I had left you.

Sir Douglas and yourself were so kind and patient with me and with the views I put forward - I am afraid somewhat inarticulately - on behalf I think I may say of the Australian public and the A.I.F. (certainly the views of the Commonwealth government) that I do hope you will allow me now to say that the removal of General Birdwood from the fighting command of the Australians would be regarded as a serious blow by the A.I.F. and the loss of his prestige in Australia would be a blow to the regard held there for the British armies.

This would be only in slight measure reduced by any arrangement the Commonwealth government might make with General Birdwood whereby he could retain his administrative functions as GOC, A.I.F. Personally I do not think any such arrangement would be made, because General Birdwood's administrative position depends upon his field command and the prestige he has created in the Force and with the public. The administrative side of his work is really little more than a D.A.G. could manage, and in any case it is the work which if the peculiar advantages of General Birdwood's position were abolished could best be done by an Australian. If we have felt our personnel weak it is not in administration, which is so entirely our domestic concern, but in senior commanders in the field.

Sentiment does not enter into the matter, or a great deal could be said about the hold that General Birdwood has established on the affections of the men here and of Australia. Australia was profoundly stirred by the Dardanelles enterprise, and gave lavishly to it in hope and spirit, as well as in material things, and it is not easy to part with these old affections.

Furthermore we would not question that in the balance of values the decision of Sir Douglas must be loyally accepted, but I do think that Australia would resent the removal of its field commander for anything else than incapacity. The effect on the troops, especially the officers, I should not like to vouch for. They are gallant fighters, but ineradically high spirited and independent.

You have impressed me on the two occasions I have had the great pleasure and profit of meeting you, as a man who respects strong opinions, fearlessly expressed. I have therefore written in this way to you, the less hesitatingly because I feel that we are devoted to common objectives and have discussed them in a frank and friendly way.

When, at the end of 1917, Haig decided to recommend William Birdwood - commander of the Australians at Anzac - for command of the Fifth British Army, Murdoch and other press correspondents talked it over in their camp in France. Murdoch accordingly went to Birdwood and told him that 'objection' would be raised to his retaining the GOC, AIF position as Army commander, at the same time assuring the general he was 'not talking for Hughes'. 'He began,' said Murdoch in rough notes he made afterwards, 'the organisation of a strong defence. He desires to retain it for prestige, for the patronage it gives him (which he loves to dispense) and for the hope of future advantage. He had then put forward a plan that "had the full support of his group", under which the whole Force would settle down and be completely Australianised.' When Murdoch was turned down he grumbled to an officer friend: 'You have, of course, long ere this heard all about the changes in the Corps. As soon as I heard of them, somewhat belatedly, I tried to get them held up . . .'

Later, discussing his Australian friend Brudenell White, a glimpse of Murdoch's dissatisfaction with Australia's traditional relationship with England could be seen. 'White is not nearly as strong in political thought as he is in military thought. He does not seem to see that the only banner under which the truly creative forces in Australia

Australian war correspondents (from left) G. L. Gilmour, Charles Bean and Keith Murdoch watching Australian battalions in action in the Hindenburg Line, France, in September 1918. (Australian War Memorial E3511)

can be collected is the banner of Australianism. He has still in him a lot of the old feeling of subservience to England which, as we both agree, cannot operate in Australia as the counterforce to Bolshevism, Sinn Feinism, and all the present disuniting, anti-Australian sections.'

As the last guns were being silenced and the enormous costs of war assessed, Murdoch looked, in letters to friends, at Australia's future . . .

> Personally I think that we will come out of the war without much material possession left for this generation, but with our eyes and hearts opened and with a tremendous driving power for the future. Let us all then get together and inspired by the single motive of a love for Australia, make our Australian democracy infinitely stronger and more powerful because of past mistakes. Germany is strong not because she is an autocracy, but because for generations her virile people have been educated in the will to power . . . I admit that democracy must be cast aside by all patriotic men if the labouring classes become selfish and indolent under the authority it gives them. That, however, is not yet the case.

And of his own future?

> To go back to Australia some day, the sooner the better, and serve her well. If I am so placed as to be permitted to use existing machinery, then all the better. When I come back I shall be prepared to renounce some things and seek the work that I can do best.
>
> Northcliffe the other day offered to find me something 'very good' in journalistic ventures for my savings. He said with my opportunities I could achieve anything, meaning that he had once stood on the same rung of the ladder. He urged me to see his Amalgamated Press manager, Sutton, and discuss what I wanted, but though possibly a fortune lies on that road I cling to Australia. The coming year is to be one of hard steady work on present lines. After that, well, I hope to get home.

6 Father and son

Keith Murdoch had caught his first sight of Lord Northcliffe, the man who was to influence his whole life, when he attended an Empire Press Union conference in 1909. Murdoch at the time was workless, self-effacing and nervous, proffering a brief letter of introduction from Alfred Deakin as his authority to attend the talks.

Northcliffe was a man of power. After *Comic Cuts* and *Answers* he had moved to bigger things and now owned the *Daily Mail* and *The Times*. Murdoch might have actually rubbed shoulders with the great man at one of the conference's social sidelights, but he turned down invitations because unhappily (he wrote to his father) he did not possess a frock-coat...

> Alfred Harmsworth (Lord Northcliffe) ... is a prominent figure. He never speaks, but his management can be detected in all the splendid arrangements for this conference. He is tall, fair with a large head and a very kindly face. He does not give an impression of great strength (although certainly strength is there) but rather a clear-sighted, deep general capability. He seems to have a great knowledge and to be simple and direct in his purposes. That, I think, is the secret of his success, if he can claim true success. He knows what he wants and goes straight for it.
>
> I expected to find him a bounding, unscrupulous showy man of the world, but he seems to be simple and kind (he wears steel-framed spectacles), and I must say I like his appearance. He now owns *The Times* as you know, and a great many London and provincial papers and one Paris paper.

Murdoch had to wait almost seven years to actually meet the man. 'When he came back from Gallipoli (Northcliffe recalled at a valedictory address to Murdoch later) he brought a dispatch, a very terrible dispatch ... he showed that dispatch to me and I suggested that the time which would be spent in carrying that ghastly record to the Antipodes could be better used for the purpose of immediate action ...'

From that moment the two got on. A journalist remembered waiting to see Northcliffe one day in an ante-room outside his office at *The Times* when 'a tall young man bustled in, said to the inquiry clerk: "Good morning. Chief in?" He knocked at Northcliffe's door and walked in. Asked who that was, the clerk replied: "That's Keith Murdoch, the Australian journalist'- a great friend of the Chief"'.

The relationship quickly developed - a dialogue and a mutual admiration between a recognised master in his profession and a young man on the threshold of what was fairly obvious to all concerned then, a spectacular newspaper career. It became such a close friendship that it firmed into almost a father-and-son relationship. Certainly

56

no newspaperman in Fleet-st. was then closer to Northcliffe than Keith Murdoch. Hurrying about *The Times* building Murdoch would chat to the Chief when he saw him about the *Herald* in Melbourne, which he was secretly planning to join. He would pick his brains about newspaper management and techniques, and about editing a paper. Murdoch was frank with his friend: he could *not* remain in London and work with him. As employer/employee they would be incompatible. Murdoch said to Theodore Fink, the *Herald's* chairman (described by one colleague as a worldly, but kindly koala): 'I feel certain that a big career is open to me here; even without entering Northcliffe's employment as he presses me to do ... I have always told you I do not want to alter my present relationship with Northcliffe. I value him as a friend, but would certainly quarrel with him as an employer. He cannot resist making his employees feel that they are the puppets of his will ... he would not permit development as I wish to develop.'

Theodore Fink, described as 'a worldly, but kindly koala', presiding over a board meeting at the Herald and Weekly Times. He wanted Murdoch to revitalise the Herald, *which was 'generating into stodge'. (Herald and Weekly Times)*

Lord Northcliffe, proprietor of The Times *and the* Daily Mail. *His close friendship with Murdoch firmed into a father-and-son relationship and his professional guidance would influence Murdoch throughout his entire career. (BBC Hulton Picture Library)*

It did not matter to Northcliffe that he had been brusquely turned down as a prospective employer. He unstintingly gave his friendship and guidance to his pupil; he told friends Murdoch had the mark of newspaper greatness. And Murdoch on his part said: 'He is the most generous man I have met in Europe.' To Northcliffe himself he said at the end of his stay in England: 'I would like to express something of my gratitude for all you have been to me since I came here four years ago. I will not say more than that you have been the biggest influence and the biggest force over me here, largely on account of the many kindnesses you have shown me, but even more largely from the example I have steadily seen in you, and the standard that you have set me. I am certainly coming back, but if I never met you again I would retain this influence to the end of my life.'

Before he left for Australia he had taken into Northcliffe a sheaf of *Heralds* and asked him to criticise them, offering his advice. He got them back and kept the Chief's comments for the rest of his life...

Make-Up:
Stop press is needed. Should be above the fold to catch the eye at once. Or it might be lateral. Must always contain some late interesting news. Size excellent. Printing good, ink very good. Make-up very bad, because advertisements dominate, and tops of columns insufficiently used. Latter point most important.
   Make far more use of pictures, especially *showing action*. Blocks are badly reproduced and insufficient. Also badly trimmed.
Advertisements:
No advertisement must dominate. It does not pay the advertiser and spoils the balance of the page. In educating the advertiser an enterprising Jew draper will be useful.
Circulation:
Net sales the foundation of a journal's power.
Staff:
A staff is like an orchestra, the editor the conductor. Find the good men on the present staff. There will certainly be one or two amongst thirty. Youth is essential, but don't get the old men against you. A cabal of that sort may be a terrible trial. Every Australian journalist should spend three years in Europe and going slowly home through America. Give holidays and rewards for good work, especially news.
Briefs:
These are valuable because they give an impression of fullness. Pack the news in: condense. Say, half a column of briefs.
   You want an appearance of fullness and intensity.
Sports:
Exploit them. Prizes and competitions: Pigeon racing (for example).
Serial:
Must be good, or useless. *Daily Mail* goes to great trouble to get the right one. Specially written round a special theme.
Women:
Run a page *every* day. Dresses, cookery, social gossip.
General:
Go very slow. You cannot run counter violently to the habits of a community. No change for three months. Spend that time going through every section, improving gradually.

Murdoch would tell how once he had sat at the feet of the great man at Northcliffe's Riviera villa where *Daily Mail* people had been invited to enjoy a 'working holiday'.

George Lambert painted this portrait of Keith Murdoch's mother, Annie Brown Murdoch, in 1927. It won the Archibald Prize.

'Landing at Anzac' by G. Lambert. Murdoch would describe the Dardanelles expedition as 'one of the most terrible chapters in our history'. *(Australian War Memorial 202)*

Page 2 of the Herald *in January 1920 – Northcliffe commented: 'make-up very bad, because advertisements dominate, and tops of columns insufficiently used.' (La Trobe collection, State Library of Victoria)*

A famous photograph – Murdoch's official farewell when he left London to take up his position as editor of the Herald. *Keith Murdoch, holding his farewell presentation golf clubs, is on Lord Northcliffe's right and Billy Hughes is on his left.*

Tom Clarke, then news editor of the *Mail*, wrote of it:

> I am sitting at the close of the day on a broad balcony. There are breakers on the beach below which cannot be seen for the intervening groves and scented gardens. A troubadour has just been singing there. Far across the bay tops of buildings and pinnacles make a fantastic mass in silhouette against the faint glow of the nearly dead day. And now little holes of light bob here and there about the falling curtain of night.
>
> Among others here is a big, hefty Australian, as jolly and mischievous as a school boy, Keith Murdoch, who directs the Australian United Cable Service in London. As he is housed in *The Times* office he comes in frequent touch with Northcliffe who has developed a warm personal regard for him; which augurs well for Murdoch's future ...

But it was not all work-talk. Northcliffe took his guests to tea at a cafe. He had no money ('Never carry it: it is a nuisance to carry.'), so Murdoch paid. 'Put it down to expenses,' said Northcliffe.

They went to the casino. Tom Clarke lost. Northcliffe said, 'Put it down to expenses, Tom.'

Back from this Riviera holiday, Murdoch wrote to Northcliffe:

> My dear Chief, I address you as such as the Chief of All Journalists (of all ages) and on returning to my desk today wished again (as I often have) that I could call you such in another way ...
>
> The days with you were complete. I have never had such a crowded and well-balanced period of enjoyment. It was the greatest privilege that any aspiring young journalist could have - one week of your company - and the actual value to me was immense. I have treasured up all you said. Moreover the setting was perfect, the company excellent and always stimulating, the period just long enough of ease and good things. We will all buckle down to hard work now with a better chance of doing things.
>
> I cannot thank you enough for this and as for the many other kindnesses you show me there is no way of showing how much I value them all. Contact with you has been one of the great things in my experience.
>
> I did not realise before the extent of your own hold on your staff. You have reduced your control of your vast organisation to a set of coherent principles which these fellows follow and understand - it makes the whole organisation coherent. By principles I mean principles of newspaper production - of the craft.

At a farewell presentation by his friends of a set of golf clubs, Murdoch took his place in the official photograph sitting next to Northcliffe, the newspaper proprietor, who was clutching a stetson and a large cigar with one hand, his spectacles, with ear-piece touching his thin mouth, in the other, a grim look frozen on a square, slightly puffy face, his hair parted almost in the middle, and carefully plastered down on his head.

7 Editor

Theodore Fink had been quietly wooing Murdoch for months. They were finally able to get together face-to-face in Melbourne when Murdoch accompanied the Prince of Wales aboard HMS *Renown* to cover the visit for a group of Australian papers and *The Times*. The Finks were going to Vancouver for an Empire Press Union conference and Murdoch was on the same ship - the *Niagara* - on his way back to London. Together they went over the *Herald* and its problems in minute detail.

Though Murdoch says he had not given Fink his decision then, it did not take him long to make up his mind to accept Fink's offer to return to Australia as editor of the *Herald* at £2,000 a year. Fink asked Murdoch his frank opinion of the 80-year-old newspaper and Murdoch replied that it had always been somewhat 'shapeless and curiously characterless as a journal ... but, of course, it is a non-competitive newspaper. It does not desire to stir up rivalries and - greatest test of all - it has been commercially successful. I have always held that a newspaper must have a fighting platform, not necessarily political, and I certainly think that the *Herald* has suffered from lack of fighting and push'.

Fink invited him to make 'any suggestions or advice you may have to offer'.

Murdoch gave it. As a broad view of the paper he wrote:

> The public attitude is for news, for bright comment, for sound and constructive criticism. Literary tone is respected: it is valuable to a newspaper, it begets a good staff ...
>
> I have much to say against stodginess, although as the Sydney *Herald* and many other newspapers prove stodginess will hold a circulation better than rocky brilliance ... I hope you will not neglect what can only be called the human side of the news and reading matter ... Human sentiment is a large part of life; rules of privacy do not debar it altogether from a newspaper, if the theme is well handled.
>
> The new form of journalism in Australia will be strong on this side. I am quite sure that some human story should be told in the *Herald* every day that every reader will read eagerly ... News - strong, dignified human handling of news - must be the postwar newspaper's chief concern.

He confessed to disappointment, later, with the *Herald* make-up: 'Not enough leads, not enough display or double column heads, lack of vigorous sub-editing ... The *Herald* is becoming very solid, but is it clever enough?'

His view of a newspaper's duty was put into a letter to Fink answering news about a quarrel between the Sydney *Sun* and a group of drapers over editorial policy as it affected their trading.

Editor – Keith Murdoch in his office at the Herald. *The farewell photograph with Lord Northcliffe takes pride of place on the wall.*

Even a struggling newspaper cannot afford to truckle to advertisers. It is wrong to do so and it does not pay. In my view the ethical and material considerations are identical. The newspaper's first consideration always is its public, which it must serve devotedly, openhandedly and with absolute loyalty. It can sell its public at any time for money, and a struggling newspaper must be sorely tempted to do so. But in that way lies not only journalistic dishonesty, degradation and treachery to all one's higher purposes in life but also material decay, for the Australian public soon finds out.

At the end of December 1920, Fink wrote to him in some consternation:

I am greatly concerned about the want of grip and appearance of the *Herald*. It is stodgy, misses a great deal and has no leadership. My six months' absence has let it slide down the hill, and it would be impossible for me always to be trying to shove it up again. The paper wants badly pulling together. We have some good writers, but they are not being made use of, and it is generating into stodge unless we get a good general.

While in America I saw the congestion in big offices in New York, Chicago, San Francisco. I warned our people to look ahead. Since my return we have decided to get a bigger site and secured an enormous block, corner Flinders, Exhibition, Little Flinders streets, and will rebuild the new premises here.

The site for the new building covered two half-acre blocks which had been bought at auction from the crown in 1838 for £166: the Flinders-st. block for £77, and the Exhibition (then Stephen)-st. block to Little Flinders-st. for £89. John Duerdin, a solicitor, built a large house, Normanhurst, on the Exhibition-st. frontage running up to Little Flinders-st. in 1857. The imposing home was set in a large garden, enclosed by a high brick wall. Duerdin lived there until 1868. A noted occupant for some years afterwards was Dr Thomas Rowan, physician and surgeon; he had his consulting rooms there.

From 1892 for some years Normanhurst was used as the Garrison Officers' mess and club. In 1896 it became Miss Bolger's boarding house, a favourite place for actors and actresses. It was still a boarding house when the Herald and Weekly Times bought the site, paying £46,000 for the two blocks.

When Murdoch arrived back in Melbourne he was installed in the old building. The editor's room was a small office, with a three-ply partition that did not reach the roof. The room was entered from a passage; over the door was a board with the word *Editor* printed on it. There was no inquiry messenger, or secretary, to find out a caller's business. One knocked on the door and was told, 'Come in.'

Murdoch sat at a plain hardwood desk on a straight-backed chair. Two or three other chairs were placed about the room: a sloping bench against a wall held newspaper files; a single window looked out over Flinders-st. Nails behind the door held coat and hat.

A friend recalls calling on him as he sat at his desk in shirt sleeves, editing a sheaf of hand-written copy; a pile of proof galleys was spiked on a corner of the desk. He had time to talk (the last edition had gone to press), and did so in an informal atmosphere, 'with the smells and sounds of a printery coming in the door. He was a brisk, well-built man, florid complexioned, eager in movement and talk'. He had been in the editor's chair only a few months. He was still feeling his way and taking time, as Northcliffe had advised, in making changes; also, he was not yet secure in his control of the paper as editor, without responsibility to the manager. He had accepted the

'Normanhurst', the gracious house built by a solicitor in 1857, which was bought by the Herald group for its new offices. For many years it was the home of the eminent physician Dr Thomas Rowan. It was last used as a boarding house. (Herald and Weekly Times)

editorship of the *Herald* without getting a clear assurance about his independence in the position, although there was an understanding that there would be no managerial interference; he had made it clear before leaving London that he was to have complete and sole control over the editorial staff, subject only to the board of directors: there should be no dictation from the managerial to the editorial side of the paper.

The new editor sitting in the stuffy little office did not have to wait long for a challenge to his authority to make decisions on editorial matters. The general manager, A.G. Wise, disputed his right to make a specific judgment. So Murdoch went to the board. 'If I don't get my way,' he said, 'I am resigning.' That board sided with him and immediately appointed him managing editor. Murdoch tapped out a letter to Northcliffe about the skirmish:

The fight with Wise was very serious, except that the Board stuck to me unanimously; he had been very jealous of the progress of the paper. You will remember you said that he would have to go and advised me to tell them to choose between us. He himself forced the fight; threatening to go on the eve of the arrival of a new evening paper, and the chief engineer saying he would go on the eve of moving into a new building and setting up a new plant which was arriving ...

Wise found the Board unanimous that he must go. He tried to make it up but I refused, and told them to choose. They chose me, so I become chief officer of the company and Wise becomes advertising manager ...

His reference to a new paper was a move from the Sydney *Sun*: even as Murdoch moved in, a rival on the Melbourne newspaper scene had been registered and staff hired - Denison had made up his mind at last to move into Victoria.

Melbourne at the time had three daily newspapers: the *Argus*, conservative, comfortably conscious of its leading place in the industry, in the number of its readers, in the quality and scope of its display advertising, and the better-class, small classified advertising; the *Age*, 'the working man's paper', second in circulation, but with a secure hold on the mass small advertising in the 'wanted to sell', situations vacant and small property classifications. Both these papers were family-owned, with simple financial structures and uncomplicated personal management. The *Herald* was the only paper financed and managed as a public company. It had a largely 'catch cash' circulation, with an advertising appeal largely in the middle-class retail market. None of the papers was technically notable, or editorially exciting. They reported happenings extensively, with routine accuracy and heavy political emphasis. They gave little attention to entertainment in reading matter.

The *Herald* was ripe for development by the time Murdoch became its chief editor, a fact that Fink had glimpsed since the war ended. It was an easy-going paper, little regarded by public men, or the reading public, for its views or for its news, comfortingly profitable, but not then a very useful medium for advertising.

The reporting staff that Murdoch took over was small, but competent. Some of the reporters were old in the paper's service, happily working at a leisurely pace. The pattern of the paper's daily appearance was set, and no event disturbed it. Special editions were rare, and the plant and presses were not equipped to meet unusual demands. The last edition of the day went to press about 4.30 pm; few reporters worked later than 4 pm. There was no urgency about news and its presentation to the public.

It was a leisurely life with the *Herald* accepting its ordained place as second to the two respectable morning papers which dully, but adequately, brought the news of the world to the breakfast table. And looking at the scene from Sydney, Denison saw the tranquil situation ripe for invasion. The *Herald*, he told his directors, was complacent and lazy. Cecil Edwards (who later became the paper's editor) said such an air of complacency hung over the *Herald* in those days that sometimes during the afternoon the head printer would appear in the sub-editors' room and announce: 'Not another line.' So far as he was concerned the paper's stomach was full. Any copy that came up to him after that time was shoved, with hardly a glance, under a lump of lead.

Murdoch rapidly began changing that slothful situation. As Northcliffe had suggested to him, he painstakingly went through every section of the *Herald* planning a new look, listing faults and omissions, and 're-jigging' pages on dummy sheets. Within a year of taking over he had put all his plans into print. Pages came alive with larger, better-planned pictures; news was written more concisely and sub-edited more drastically; advertisement layouts had more thought given to them and less of the heavy black type that had so horrified Northcliffe.

Then Murdoch turned to his staff. A sensitive man himself, Keith Murdoch saw reporters not as word-machines or clerks who could type reams of noted facts, but as vulnerable, temperamental personalities who would respond to being noticed and to being given a little kindness. He began seeking them out in the reporters' room, chatting about their daily assignments, their hopes, their reading, their mortgages, their families. He prided himself on not only knowing their names but their wives' names and occasionally the names of their children.

At work on the site of the new Herald *building. The land, which fronted onto Flinders, Exhibition and Little Flinders streets, was bought for £46,000. (Herald and Weekly Times)*

Those who responded to the big man's interest found themselves caught up in his enthusiasm for news and the profession of newspapers and were stimulated to greater effort; those who cynically suspected the new thrust he was making fell quickly by the wayside. Murdoch was laying down a whole new genetic strain of Australian newspapermen: *the Murdoch Man*. Such a man would be infected with the eager, bright-eyed enthusiasm of his chief; he would respond to a 'Well done!' or the occasional congratulatory note – or to a bonus slipped (a little more rarely) into his pay packet. The Murdoch Man's pride was big enough to deflect the sneers of those in the office who objected to the new broom disturbing them, and to the jibes of those on rival newspapers who were sarcastic about what was happening in Flinders-st., but who secretly wished they were part of it.

As he made his way through the *Herald* or interviewed people in his office, Keith Murdoch still experienced difficulty in communicating. Mr Lionel Logue, the Australian therapist who had done such good work with King George VI's stutter, had been consulted and had improved Murdoch's too; but he still spoke badly in public and the shyness which overcame him when he sought to bare his soul in private was painfully apparent. It was a handicap, but it did not prevent him inspiring his men; rather they admired him more for battling it.

The revitalised newspaper they were producing was now ready for any attack from a new contender for the evening sales crown. Murdoch had always expected such a move would come from Sydney and that it would come from Denison's Sydney *Sun*. Hugh Denison had made no secret of his aspirations in Melbourne and had warned Murdoch, long before, that he would enter the morning paper field first and then switch over to an evening paper. Murdoch replied that such a move would be 'suicidal'.But Denison knew the *Sun* with its brash outlook on Sydney life was swamping the more timid *Evening News* and he could see no reason why the same formula would not take readers away from the pedantic sheets offered in Melbourne.

When Murdoch realised how serious Denison was about opening in opposition he made a hurried trip north and began a secret swoop on the shares of the struggling *Evening News*. He would take the newspaper over himself, he had decided, and give Denison a battle to fight in his own back yard. But a domestic squabble over advertising spiked Murdoch's guns. A group of Sydney drapers had become incensed with an announced advertising rate increase planned by the *Sun* and made up their minds to give Denison's paper a little opposition. They provided a much-needed influx of capital for the *Evening News* so the *Sun* might think twice about its complacent attitude towards its advertisers. Murdoch turned back, and had not settled in his office long when the invader arrived. The *Sun* organisation launched the *Sun News-Pictorial* on to Melbourne's morning streets in September 1922. It was a tabloid, modelled on London's *Daily Sketch* and *Daily Mirror*, and four of its twenty pages were given over to pictures. Montague Grover was to be the editor and was also named as editor of 'the coming evening paper'. It was Melbourne's first new daily newspaper in thirty-one years.

The *Sun News-Pictorial's* appeal to the younger Melbourne reader was instant. Nobody had offered them much before; the *Argus*, recalled Cecil Edwards, 'looked and read as if it was produced by the Melbourne Club for the Melbourne Club'. The *Age* had become querulous and doddery in its outlook, with turgid writing; and who could get a sense of urgency from a front page made up of classified ads? Neither paper had appeal for the young at heart. The *Sun News-Pictorial* did. It was a handy size, its pages were packed with pictures and its accent was on human interest.

Only a few weeks after the *Herald* had moved to its new plant, the *Evening Sun* was launched as Denison had threatened. It was coloured pink; it was sensational and it set out immediately to pick at little faults in the *Herald*, breaking the old 'dog-doesn't-eat-dog' rule newspapers had traditionally followed. With all its cheekiness and brashness the *Evening Sun* did not click with the Melbourne evening paper reader. Within two years it had decided to pack up, and only after its demise did Murdoch deign to mention its existence in the *Herald* columns.

His Northcliffe-style expertise adapted to Australian conditions had pushed the *Herald* circulation upwards during the fight from 120,000 to 137,000. And soon after the *Evening Sun* was laid to rest the *Herald* was selling 175,000.

In its final death throes Montague Grover had written to Murdoch:

> Dear Keith, The Board has instructed me to draft the following notice for insertion in the Pictorial tomorrow morning:
> Important Announcement
> Owing to the great expense of production, the *Evening Sun* will be published today for the last time.
> The *Sun News-Pictorial* has been sold at a thoroughly satisfactory figure to the Herald Proprietary, by whom it will be taken over at an early date. Full particulars will appear in this afternoon's *Evening Sun*.

A few hours before the *Evening Sun* made its abrupt exit from Melbourne's newspaper world Theodore Fink signed a statement that was circulated to the Herald's shareholders informing them that the directors of the company had purchased the *Sun News-Pictorial* 'on what they consider satisfactory terms. The transaction relates to the *Sun News-Pictorial* aone, and the price paid is based on the actual value and earning power of that journal'.

Rumours about the impending end of the *Evening Sun* had caused a rise in the market price of Herald shares, but Fink warned that in the directors' opinion this rise 'was not justified by any expectation of corresponding increases in rate of dividends or other distributions to our shareholders'.

The company paid (as the financial price of the *Evening Sun* ceasing to exist) £175,000 for the copyright and goodwill of the illustrated tabloid, and some newsprint stocks. Plant and real estate were not included in the deal.

Sir Hugh Denison in a published statement on 25 April announcing the end of the *Evening Sun* said the *News-Pictorial* had achieved 'financial success', but the loss on the *Evening Sun* had 'nullified this feat'. The *Sun* was discontinuing publication 'in the interests of its shareholders'.

The total loss on the operation of the evening paper was estimated at between £200,000 and £300,000.

Negotiations for the taking over of the *Sun News-Pictorial* were carried out by Keith Murdoch. This was for him the fruits of a personal triumph; victory over a formidable opponent. He was excited about it, for it established his place in the newspaper industry and it confirmed his authority as the managing editor of the Herald and Weekly Times' publications.

The failure of the *Evening Sun* had dealt a severe blow at workers in the newspaper industry, journalists, technicians, compositors, printers, advertising, commercial and publishing staffs. The industry was just emerging from a depression that had followed upon a postwar boom. It was the greatest disaster since the Melbourne *Herald* had taken over, and closed, the *Evening Standard* in the late 1890s.

The best of the *Sun's* staff went to the Melbourne *Herald* and the *Sun News-Pictorial* staffs. That left many still on the labour market. The company established funds (to which Sydney Sun Newspapers Ltd. contributed) to help men until they could find new work. These funds were administered by the journalists' and printers' unions. They softened the economic blow, and most of the displaced workers found new work within a year.

In 1921 Lord Northcliffe had become ill and there was concern among his friends and family for his nervous state. He was advised by his doctors to take a long sea voyage and rest, so he told Murdoch he would be dropping into Melbourne. The delighted Murdoch saw to it that 'The Chief' was introduced to all his friends and colleagues and was taken to important dinner parties attended by men who might influence Murdoch's career. A member of the wealthy Baillieu family chatted to Northcliffe at one of these dinners and asked 'how one made money in newspapers'. Northcliffe replied: 'There is only one way, you have to back the man. And this young Murdoch is someone to back.' ('They took his word for it,' said Rupert Murdoch half a century later. 'They bought shares in the *Herald* and supported him in his takeover of the Adelaide *Advertiser*.')

Murdoch made sure 'The Chief' had a sheaf of *Heralds* to take aboard ship when he departed from Melbourne and more sent on to await his arrival in Colombo. Northcliffe read them carefully and sent back detailed critical notes. 'The letters to the editor are good. People like to read about profiteers. Most of them would like to be profiteers themselves, and would be if they had the chance.

'The church notes were good. People who drink, smoke and swear have no idea of the interest in church matters. Australians told me the contrary, but I prefer to use the evidence of my own eyes. I saw plenty of church and chapel going on Sundays in Australia.' He counselled Murdoch: 'Ask your father about it. He will not be an unbiased witness, naturally, but knows a great deal more about it than a newspaper reporter.'

'The Chief' still detested the use of large black type in advertisements. Newspapers of the time in Australia were stridently overburdened with it to advertise wares that ranged from silks to ironmongery. He told Murdoch: 'You can't be as independent as I am, and your public is rather like ours of twenty years ago - used to the larger type. Personally, if I were printing the *Herald* I should kick out such advertisements . . . that mass of black gives your picture printer a rare job. Does the picture editor understand printing machines? I make mine go down and stand by them and see what part of the block hits the paper . . . He should have long confabs with the printing press man, whom he should ply with drink occasionally and take to his bosom generally. These twain can help the editor a lot.'

Northcliffe had made a ritual of writing daily notes to his staffs, praising or condemning what they had done that day with his newspapers. He had given Murdoch a pile of them before he left England and now Murdoch began the same practice. His 'Editor's Notes' started in February 1924; they were drafted at home and then dictated to a secretary; they critically examined how the *Herald* had handled crime, advertising, religion, gambling . . .

Soon after Murdoch took over as editor the Herald *had been transformed. There was a stronger emphasis on pictures and concise news and advertisements no longer dominated the pages. By 1922 the circulation had been boosted from 120,000 to 175,000. (La Trobe collection, State Library of Victoria)*

On advertisements:

We must wean advertisers away from dense smudges of ink and induce them to accept pyramid placings of advertisements to carry the reader with feelings of surprise and interest through all pages. Headlines should tell the news sharply, tersely ...

On gambling:

The sound rule in betting is to star betting failures and minimise successes. We do harm by featuring betting successes, good by featuring betting failures. (Sir Keith was always strongly against gambling. But he would take overseas visitors to the Melbourne Cup. 'They would be lining up at the £20 and £10 windows at the Tote,' said his son, 'and Father would be at the £1 window making his big bet of the year.')

On Melbourne:

The paper has Melbourne's character tonight, not brilliant, not intensely pointed, but kindly, efficient and very sound.

On crime:

When we must give space to a horror, all other horrors in the paper should be kept very brief indeed.

Though Keith Murdoch's routing of the brash Sydney invader had given him an enhanced respect in the eyes of his board he could not afford to sit back on his laurels; he was to face two more scraps.

The first was little more than a skirmish. The Victorian Farmers' Union had often dreamed of a daily newspaper that would, above all, serve country interests. The Union had formed Victorian Newspapers Ltd. with small parcels of shares sold to investors and farmers and it enabled the company to purchase the old Flinders-st. offices that had previously been home for the *Herald*. On 29 October 1925, the *Morning Post* went on sale at one penny – a halfpenny cheaper than its rivals. It was not only to battle its established competitors but be disturbed by squabbles amongst those who controlled it and it died two years later with a circulation that had never exceeded 50,000. It was sold to Pictorial Newspapers Pty Ltd., the registered publisher of the *Sun News-Pictorial* for £31,000. Shareholders – many of them struggling farmers who could ill-afford it – lost 12/- in the £1 subscribed.

Murdoch's second fight was set down for early 1933 as the world was dragging itself painfully out of the Great Depression. New hope and some confidence were beginning to be sensed in the business world and the *Argus* directors secretly decided it was a good time to launch an evening paper to oppose the *Herald*. Emissaries were dispatched to have furtive discussions at their homes and out-of-the-way hotel bars with key *Herald* staff men and plans for the *Star* were quietly outlined. Top *Herald* men like Cecil Edwards, Allan Burbury and Jack Waters – Murdoch Men to a man – were approached, and to the amazement of colleagues who got to hear about it they agreed to offer themselves on a battleground already strewn with bleaching bones from previous evening-sales wars.

Why should they have done so? They were working for the best evening newspaper in Australia and arguably one of the finest newspaper operators in the world. Why risk their futures?

Frederick Howard, for many years a senior *Herald* feature writer and leader writer who stood on the sidelines, believed it was because they were *bored*. 'It wasn't so much the higher money, because the *Argus* was never noted for its lavish spending; it was the lure of something new.' Cecil Edwards recalled he had always been told by Murdoch 'A man must reach executive rank by the time he is thirty if he is to get anywhere

in newspapers'. Well, Edwards was perilously close to thirty and saw no immediate prospect of *Herald* executive rank, so he handed in his notice. 'When Murdoch heard about it,' recalls Howard, 'he was furious. He had them all in and made a dramatic speech which he concluded by saying: "... and never darken my doorstep again."' He was concerned not so much about the challenge from the *Argus* (which was on the verge of bankruptcy) but that his 'young men' should desert him with their talents and their loyalty. Murdoch angrily decided to post Waters off to Darwin as the *Herald* representative so he could not, during his period of notice, give any of his talents to the *Star*. But Waters point-blank refused to go and was summarily dismissed for having refused a duty. Murdoch said plaintively to Cecil Edwards when he came to say goodbye: 'Why are all my young men leaving me?' (It was a wistful question that was to be repeated to this writer by Waters himself, returned and executive-crowned thirty years later.) When Cecil Edwards had settled in at the *Star* to be its chief sub-editor he had been appalled to see the incompetence, lack of money, lack of understanding of evening paper operation and sheer ignorance, all of which, he said, combined to bring about the predictable death of the semi-tabloid pictorial. Its first issue on 30 October 1933 was a mess. The *Star* lasted for two years and five months and then it blinked out. Murdoch forgave his young men and they were allowed not only to darken the doorstep, but to re-cross it and return to the fold.

There were two persistent, ugly rumours over the years about the death of the *Star*: one that Murdoch had sent his bright young men over *to sabotage it*; the second that the *Herald* had offered the *Argus* a price to close down the rival. Both were groundless. No money or sabotage expertise would have been needed - sheer managerial incompetence did the job as conclusively as any saboteur could have done. Edwards, who returned to later become editor of the *Herald*, made a point before he died of denying taking part in any sabotage plan. He wrote in his book *The Editor Regrets*:

> I must refer here to a persistent belief that Murdoch played a Machiavellian part in the *Star's* failure. It was published in the Communist weekly, the *Guardian*, and is still repeated. This is a slander that I specifically deny. No worse slur could be on men's professional reputations than to say they deliberately pulled the plug out of the craft they were engaged to navigate ... the paper was sabotaged, but by managerial ineptitude and scarcity of money. The people who tried to save it from the results of incompetence were those who, according to the rumour, were inserted there to wreck it. That the *Herald* should offer us jobs while the *Star* was staggering seems to me to be good business. Why not grab good newspapermen while they are available, and at the same time deal what may be (and was) a fatal blow?

Before the *Sun News-Pictorial* was tucked under Murdoch's wing he had been made editor-in-chief and was now at the helm of 1,000 people producing newspapers and magazines in Flinders-st. Somehow, though, the magic the burly man with the quizzical eyebrows brought to daily newspapers was notably absent when he turned his mind to a magazine.The first glossy he was to mastermind was *Punch*, an amalgamation of *Melbourne Punch* and *Table Talk*, two venerable journals that offered chatty political, social and theatrical gossip, with cartoons and caricatures stirred in with photographs, sport and mild scandal. The first number of *Punch* that came out at the end of 1924 was pretentious, dull and fatuous. It went under quickly.

Murdoch also controlled another magazine, one which he neither wanted nor had had any part in buying. It was *Stead's Revue*, which had been started in World War 1 and came out fortnightly. During hostilities it had a big circulation among people keen to know the 'inside story' of what was going on in the war, which it told expertly, drawing on good sources, causing headaches among the censors. Then it dropped away over the years and began losing circulation, finding itself in the possession of the printers to whom it owed a lot of money. Shabby now, and spiritless, it still managed to come out and one day it caught the eye of Theodore Fink who had always nurtured a desire to publish a literary, iconoclastic review. Fink cast his eyes a little ambitiously towards America's *Atlantic Monthly* as an example of what he wanted. He had been told *Stead's Revue* had a circulation of 5,000 and he bought it while Murdoch was abroad on business. In fact it sold half that number and things were much worse than Fink had believed. He put young Frederick Howard, a newcomer to the *Herald* staff, in charge as editor and hoped Howard could transform his purchase.

' "K.M." came back from overseas,' said Howard, 'and found his company committed to this wretched little magazine. It had been bought without consulting him at all and he was furious! It widened a rift which had already opened between he and Fink. The magazine struggled through the Depression and then it was sold to a Sydney group who turned it into a news digest. "K.M." barely tolerated it while the *Herald* owned it and of course it was a rather inauspicious start to my career with him.'

Churned out on the Flinders-st. presses was yet another magazine called *Pal*, which was supposed to be a bright, fun publication that would specifically interest schoolboys. 'It was run by two doddering old gentlemen,' remembers Howard. 'One had been in charge of a Sunday school and the other was a very zealous, but not particularly bright, naturalist. Like the rest, it faded away.'

8 The girl in the magazine

Murdoch, the 43-year-old newspaper 'genius' might well have been maladroit at producing magazines, but he was to live to be grateful for owning one of them. One morning a photograph scheduled for his *Table Talk* was put on his desk for approval and it introduced him to the girl he was to marry.

He had for two years lived as a bachelor in a serviced flat at Cliveden, East Melbourne, a respectable establishment which was home or *pied-a-terre* to dowagers and retired squatters. But as demands on him to return hospitality and entertain visitir g business leaders increased, he decided to move to a house in Walsh-st., South Yarra, where, after a busy day in Flinders-st., he could arrive home to find his clothes laid out by servants for his next appointment, or a dinner party prepared over which he would preside.

He was paying attention at the time to Peggy Ainslie Mills, the daughter of a well-known Riverina merino stud family. When Peggy became ill with a serious and medically perplexing spinal complaint Murdoch was constantly at her bedside, comforting her. They became engaged. But later, as the prospect of Peggy's recovery strengthened, the two realised they were not meant for each other and they agreed to break off the engagement.

Murdoch resumed his Melbourne social life as an interesting, personable bachelor; but increasing pressure of his newspaper responsibilities was making him reluctant to accept too many invitations to dinners and parties. He was handsome, well-mannered and comfortably off; mothers in the Toorak-South Yarra area saw him as a particularly good 'catch'. As their daughters made their way through the season and 'came out' into society, there was gentle elbowing for the attention of this brilliant newspaper editor. One day, in 1927, he was asked by a matron he knew if he would attend a charity ball in Toorak; Murdoch's immediate reaction was to decline. He had a busy time ahead of him that particular week and he was still shy at meeting people personally (as distinct from interviewing them professionally, when his awkwardness quickly left him and his probing became forthright and intense, with no sign at all of his stammer). Then he heard the lady mention *debutantes*, and somehow that rang a bell. He had just seen an extraordinarily pretty, striking face in *Table Talk* just before it went to press ... a *debutante* called Elisabeth Greene. Would there be any chance, he wondered, that Miss Greene would be at the ball? Yes, enthused the matron, she would! Ah, well, said Murdoch, in that case he might be able to, ah ... re-arrange his diary. 'I will come,' he said, with a smile, 'if you will promise to introduce me to Miss Elisabeth Greene.'

There was something about this bright, happy face in his magazine that stirred him even more as he looked at it again. He put on his dinner-suit that evening and drove

Murdoch was 43 years old when this issue of Table Talk *was placed on his desk for approval. It introduced him to Miss Elisabeth Greene, the girl he was to marry. (La Trobe collection, State Library of Victoria)*

to the ball where the amused social dignitary who had invited him kept her bargain and led him across to meet Miss Elisabeth Greene. She was indeed beautiful, amusing – and just 18. The two spoke briefly and politely, then parted without Murdoch getting up the courage to ask her to dance. Nevertheless he hardly took his eyes from the girl the whole evening. 'These big, dark compelling eyes just followed me around the room,' said Elisabeth. 'It was a very significant night.'

Murdoch found time in his busy schedule at the *Herald* next day to discover the Greenes' telephone number and he telephoned to ask Elisabeth if she thought she might possibly like to drive down to the beach at Sorrento with him the following weekend? 'I said "yes", but I got into terrible hot water over it. My family were fairly old-fashioned and they thought a young girl going out for the day with a man of 43 in a motor-car was absolutely unheard of! But it *was* the twenties after all, and Keith's circle of friends were a gay lot.' It was the age of the Hesitation Waltz, the Charleston; orchestras playing romantic melodies like 'Valencia' and 'Smile a While' as shingled flappers melted into strong male arms . . .

'My sisters, who were older than I, also took a rather anxious view of it. There was a family discussion and it was decided that I *might* be able to go if it were found out who else was going. This was reported back to Keith, and Lady Gullett was roped in to be our chaperone. My family did not know Keith, but one of my sisters who was awfully shy, had recently sat next to him at a dinner party and he had been kind to her. So there was now a tiny gleam of approval.'

Sorrento was 'select' and dignified. The better-off people owned seaside houses, or took them for the school holidays. Some stayed at the hotel overlooking the sea. The trip down there for the day in Murdoch's gleaming 1926 model car, the elfin-faced, intelligent girl beside him, was a journey he would never forget. Lady Gullett did her best not to intrude, and as they tramped over the sands past the bathing-boxes Keith resolved to himself that this was indeed a friendship that should be nurtured. He asked Elisabeth if she might be allowed to join a weekend house-party at Sorrento, bringing her elder sister, Marie, down as well, to stay with some of his friends?

The Greenes, having met him and sensed an earnestness and trustworthiness, surprisingly agreed. In a few months Murdoch asked Elisabeth if she would marry him.

'It caused a terrific rumpus,' Dame Elisabeth said. 'My parents had great pressure brought to bear on them from old friends who were very fond of me. I had one

Sorrento, the pretty beach resort on Victoria's Mornington Peninsula, attracted many Melbourne people for weekend visits. (La Trobe collection, State Library of Victoria)

generous, kind godfather who had been very good to me and who had helped educate me; when the discussion about it took place with him there was an awful scene. It looked as though I wasn't going to get my way. But my mother and father saw that Keith was good; they knew that I was strong-minded and so they allowed our engagement.

'Looking back on it, I just think how extraordinary it was that I - at 18 - had the cheek to believe I could be adequate.'

She was being asked to become the wife of one of Melbourne's most successful business-men, hostess at a table at which the great were asked to dine. And many of her husband's friends would be older than her by 30 or 40 years . . .

They married, and Elisabeth Murdoch's first dinner party threw her into confusion; she had no idea how to correctly place four married couples around the table so that husband was not sitting next to wife. 'Keith liked everything to be just perfect, but he was wonderfully patient. When I made a rather slapdash job of the tea-pouring ceremony, which he liked to be just right, Lady Gullett noticed Keith's consternation and said: "Look at poor Keith and his tea; he's going through absolute agony. There's no ceremony about you, darling . . ." '

When Keith Murdoch had met Elisabeth Greene he felt his life was overflowing

with happiness. 'I think he really wanted very much to get married,' she said. 'He was such a kind man, he loved family and children so much ... and he was furnishing his own house. He had been terribly hard-up in his young days and he had a great sense of responsibility towards his own family. I think he hadn't got time enough for romance.'

On the eve of their tenth wedding anniversary Keith wrote to Elisabeth on a train to Adelaide:

> This is your special tenth anniversary letter but it is quite hard to write because the subject needs hundreds of pages and a lot of time. I can't begin to explain how I feel about these ten happy years and all the wonderful things you have done for me and how really wonderful I think you are. It was an amazing piece of luck for me that you were just you, because I could not have been so happy with anyone else. I know how much I must have tried you, but I've always been deeply in love with you and adore you more than ever. In addition to which your loveliness is even greater in maturity than as sweet and pretty nineteen, or Heavens, was it eighteen?'

Before their marriage, Keith Murdoch had bought Home Farm, a property near Langwarrin, down the Port Phillip bay coast 30 miles from Melbourne. There was a substantial weatherboard house on about 90 acres of land fronting Cranbourne road, a few miles from seaside Frankston. This became their joy for the remainder of Keith's life. There was a charm of paddock, old trees, sandy rides through tea-tree clumps, and a quiet, farm-like atmosphere. They re-named it Cruden Farm.

The year after he and Elisabeth were married, Murdoch had become managing director of The Herald and Weekly Times Ltd. and in this year the company recorded its

Murdoch's first step towards personal financial interest in newspapers came in 1926 when he led a syndicate which took over the West Australian *in Perth.*

first profit exceeding £200,000. Under his leadership the *Herald* had bought radio station 3DB and was the first Australian newspaper to enter the broadcasting industry.

Murdoch had already taken his first steps towards personal financial interest and control of newspapers. His first target was Perth's *West Australian*. He led a syndicate which included W.L. Baillieu, an investor who had been a childhood friend, W.S. Robinson, with whom he had worked on the *Age* many years ago, Theodore Fink, and the board of The Herald and Weekly Times. They took the paper over and made it into a public company, West Australian Newspapers Ltd., in September 1926. Murdoch then turned his attention to the Adelaide newspaper scene. The *Adelaide Register* was the State's oldest paper and was ailing. It was heavily overshadowed by the *Advertiser* which was solid, though unadventurous, but had a State-wide sale. Murdoch's syndicate bought it in 1928 and turned the broadsheet into a semi-tabloid pictorial, shaking the circulation up from 6,000 to 14,000 in a few months. Why on earth did they want the old *Register*, people asked? There was a very good reason. Murdoch had his eyes on the *Advertiser*, which was owned by a tenacious, extremely wealthy octogenarian, Sir Langdon Bonython, who had edited the *Advertiser* for the last thirty-one years, and who looked askance at the facelift his paper's rival was getting. Then to worry him even more, Murdoch dropped the price of the *Register* to one penny. Sir Langdon gave in to the pressure and agreed to sell the *Advertiser* to the syndicate for £1 million. But even after the takeover and the formation of Advertiser Newspapers Ltd. the old man could not allow himself to let go, and continued to come into the paper and work every night as if he were still editor. He had been appointed chairman of directors, but instead of remaining decorative - as was his role so far as the syndicate was concerned - he threatened to obstruct changes. He was only persuaded to step aside after he was promised the right to come into the office daily and supervise the leading articles. When Sir Langdon died, he left an estate of £4 million.

Murdoch recognised that improvement was urgently needed in all departments of the *Advertiser* but it would have to be done deftly without upsetting the touchy South Australian readers. The *Register* was stagnating; the Depression had shaken it so badly financially that in 1931 it was decided to close it down.

Keith Murdoch then began making long train journeys north to Brisbane. The first newspaper published in that city was the *Moreton Bay Courier* which had been changed to the *Courier* in 1861 (when it became a daily) and then to the *Brisbane Courier* three years later. Its rival, the *Daily Mail*, had been first published in 1903 and twelve years later was bought by John Wren, a wealthy Melbourne investor with interests in many fields including land and racing. Murdoch had noticed in the late 1920s that the *Daily Mail* was also feeling the pinch of the Depression and he talked to Wren about shaking it up. Wren agreed it needed help and sold Murdoch a share in the paper. The two never became close in their partnership and dealt with the business of control by letter.

It was soon obvious that there was little room for competing morning daily newspapers in Brisbane. Both the *Courier* and the *Mail* were facing rising costs and production problems, so when a surviving owner of the *Courier* agreed to sell it to Murdoch he and Wren decided to close the *Mail* and merge it with the *Courier*. They formed Queensland Newspapers Ltd. and published the first issue of the *Courier-Mail* on 28 August 1933. For the first time Keith Murdoch held a controlling personal interest in a newspaper. He had the right to nominate the entire board of directors during his lifetime and spend up to £50,000 without consulting a general meeting of all classes of shareholders.

Further newspaper purchases initiated by Murdoch followed, including the Advertiser *in Adelaide, the old* Moreton Bay Courier *and* Daily Mail *in Brisbane, and the* News *in Adelaide.*

In the heart of the Depression – a rally by the unemployed in Perth in 1931. There were several clashes with police (West Australian)

Though The Herald and Weekly Times was often – sometimes disparagingly – called 'The Murdoch Press', Murdoch was never to have more than a few shares in the company. He controlled it and its many publications when he was made chairman of directors, but his personal fortunes were not involved. *He had other ideas …*

While he was making his frequent trips to Adelaide masterminding the purchase of the *Advertiser*, he pondered on the long train journey about Adelaide's afternoon newspaper, the *News*. Might it become a thorn in the *Advertiser's* side one day? There had already been whispers of a Sydney invasion and Murdoch had experienced the resultant problems such circulation battles caused. So he went to the owners of the *News* and put a 'mutual-protection' case to them. There was, as a result, an agreed exchange of shares between News Ltd. and the newly formed Advertiser Newspapers

Ltd. which gave both newspapers a better feeling of security against any potential attack. The share-swop carried no voting rights on either side, at the time. But the Depression forced a re-thinking. The *News* was now in trouble. It found it could not meet mortgage debentures or pay preference dividends; the money was just not coming in fast enough. The *Advertiser* and the Herald and Weekly Times stepped in and met all the commitments of the *News*. In return for this Murdoch demanded - and got - voting rights for the *Advertiser's* shares, giving him actual control of the *News*. It meant he had a monopoly control of the press in Adelaide.

The Herald and Weekly Times soon held just under half the total shareholding of News Ltd., and at the same time controlled 114,000 *Advertiser* shares that were held by News Ltd. This therefore gave the Herald and Weekly Times nearly two-thirds ownership in Advertiser Newspapers Ltd. Murdoch's personal power was now strong: he was chairman of directors and managing director of The Herald and Weekly Times, and chairman of directors of Advertiser Newspapers Ltd. And the shareholding strength of those companies gave him actual control of News Ltd. *He was now, without doubt, the most powerful newspaper controller in Australia.* As he stepped to the *Herald* chairmanship he was also the largest individual shareholder in Queensland Newspapers Ltd.

Murdoch was knighted during that year, for services to journalism, having twice before turned down knighthoods offered by Lloyd George and Billy Hughes.

In the early thirties the Murdochs' Walsh-st. residence was steadily becoming a salon of some distinction. At its table could be found generals, prime ministers, art experts and sometimes the humble reporter who had been summoned to break bread with the big man.

Murdoch had become intensely interested in fine art, silver, and good furniture. He had an excellent library. Manservants waited at his table and his door was opened by a butler. 'Yet,' says Frederick Howard, 'he didn't seem to be quite at home with his wealth and power. He kept up a considerable style, and would come into the office on Saturday mornings in riding breeches and cravat, having exercised early on the tan in Alexandra Avenue. There seemed to be a half-desire to play "the squire", but with it all he was rather self-conscious. Elisabeth was also a sweet and natural person and I'm not sure she enjoyed it an awful lot either.'

Murdoch now had an ever-increasing obsession with quality; quality in his papers, quality in his men, quality in politicians; quality in his home and in his surroundings; quality in works of art; quality in his dress - the beautifully tailored tweed, the shoes, the carefully chosen tie - all bought at the right place. Even the little pigskin diary he carried, and the properly conservative make of car. Quality in his hotels - Claridges, and the currently fashionable restaurants, the Trocadero and Ciro's. 'He *enjoyed* good things, not only because they were costly and perhaps enviable, but mainly for their intrinsic worth and beauty,' says Douglas Brass. 'It was partly, perhaps, a compensation for the lean years. But it was also a reflection of his cosmopolitan ways and his vast experience - and I fancy, also, his hurry to catch up with life and graciousness in middle age. There was something of acquisitiveness in it, too. But his instinct for quality must have been inborn. Rich men accumulate possessions, but few with the discrimination and taste that Murdoch showed. He loved beautiful things just as he loved the good use of the English language. He was a perfectionist - and lucky, and indeed *innocent*, enough to experience a little perfection in an ugly world.'

Murdoch's business interests were spreading from newspaper direction and ownership to the need to establish an Australian newsprint industry in case of world shortages or war. He resolved to take steps to set up a pulp mill for The Herald and Weekly Times, and hoped he could interest other newspapers to 'come in' with him. After experimenting with eucalypts from forest leases in Tasmania, success came in 1934.

Australian-produced newsprint was used for the first time in 1941 to print a paper, the Hobart *Mercury*. It was dark brown in colour and it crumbled easily. Sir Lloyd Dumas, an Adelaide newspaper executive, said: 'How the *Mercury* machine crew got it through their presses we could not understand.' Murdoch had worked tirelessly to get squabbling newspaper interests to invest with him in the industry and at last saw his project come to fruition. He reported to his board during the early part of the war that Tasmanian newsprint was now of good quality and was 'a lifesaver to the Australian newspapers'. There was not an Australian publisher, he said after the war, who could have weathered the war without it.

The first aerial newspaper deliveries started in the late 1920s. The first Herald *delivery to Canberra was made by this Qantas aeroplane. (Herald and Weekly Times)*

9 A mistake

For a young editor, Keith Murdoch had, long before he took the chair, a unique grounding in the machinery and personalities in politics. His Gallipoli letter had thrust him into the highest British political circles; his early reporting of Parliament in Melbourne and the later use Hughes made of him in London gave him an intimacy with Australia's political leaders few reporters could have dreamed of enjoying.

He revelled in the intrigue; he liked the sudden excitement, the angry exchanges and the hot blood of warring personalities. He liked to be 'in the know' during the decision-making. And it would have been an extraordinary man controlling more newspaper voices than any other person in the land who would not have enjoyed the heady power of the printed word.

Yet Harold Cox, who was in charge of the *Herald's* Canberra bureau for many years and was one of Murdoch's political 'ears', said: 'He had, of course, strong views on many controversial matters and he never hesitated to declare these. He frequently stated these views in articles published under his own name. But it would have been unthinkable for Murdoch to want some politician singled out for abuse, belittling or, by omission, cast into obscurity. He liked to play a part in shaping things, and I think he got a kick out of participation in public affairs. He had ideas of his own and he wanted to have them ventilated widely; for instance, he wanted to improve relations with America.'

He was also wary now of politicians 'using' *him*.

Murdoch had not long been editor when his old chief-user Hughes came to the end of the road as Prime Minister. There had by now been a painful change in their relationship and Murdoch had warned his *Herald* staff in a memorandum: 'We should be careful of W.M. Hughes. His motives are ugly - vindictiveness, jealousy, self-interest. His dominant idea is not to help the country but to destroy Bruce (who was to succeed Hughes as Prime Minister).' As the shadows of the widening depression threatened Australia, Murdoch began to think about national policy. When he had come to the chair the *Herald* was of little political consequence and he had worked to build it as a newspaper rather than a journal of opinion. He determined to change this. Canberra was now the seat of politics and he opened a bureau there soon after Parliament's first sessions began.

It became painfully obvious soon after the world slump began that Australia was in for some severe belt-tightening to enable it to pay interest on debts to Britain, and a leading Bank of England economist travelled out to assess the situation. He advised severe slashing of production costs and government expenditure. Murdoch made up

The Herald *subs' room in 1927 - Keith Murdoch worked the subs hard when he took over as editor, demanding sharper editing and better page layouts. (Herald and Weekly Times)*

his mind that as an individual, and as a controller of newspapers, he would bear a share of the discomfort. He asked employees for acceptance of a wage cut of 10 per cent of earnings. But the Australian Journalists' Association said the employers should take the proper step of asking the Arbitration Court to vary the agreement which existed between journalists and proprietors. The employers' representative who had made the approach said this was not acceptable; the employers would not like it to be thought they were breaking the agreement.

The Herald and Weekly Times then took a further step to resolve this position by issuing notices of dismissal to every employee, those notices to editorial department employees were signed by the managing director, Keith Murdoch. No explanation was given.

A week later the Australian Journalists' Association, Victoria District, held a special meeting which agreed, not without acrimony and by a small majority, to offer a 10 per cent reduction in the wages that had been fixed by agreement. All the notices of dismissal of the Herald and Weekly Times were withdrawn.

Murdoch gave the picture of depression at the *Herald* in the internal news-sheet *House News* in February 1931, explaining the steps that had been taken to meet the grim economic conditions. He wrote, 'We have lost 30 per cent of our advertising revenue, more than £200,000 a year, and on that figure the increased cost of duty and exchange will be £120,000.' The pay cut over all employees, he added, averaged 13 per cent. He claimed this was generally less than in other sections of industry throughout Australia. The company's directors had taken a cut of 20 per cent. Executives in addition to a percentage cut in salaries had lost much of their bonus. Throughout the firm, pay reductions had contributed £50,000 a year.

Murdoch pushed his ideas for economic stability hard. He attacked the Labor Party - particularly hitting at extremists in the industrial and political wings. The Trades Hall Council angrily responded by calling for a ban on his newspapers and the ejection of the *Herald* representative from Council meetings. There was a march through the city of unemployed men carrying banners and shouting slogans; when they reached the *Herald* building they paused to give three groans. Murdoch's involvement with the economic crisis became more passionate as newspapers took sides in the search for an answer; his objectivity as a reporter was often nudged aside by his passion as a propagandist for his point of view. He believed in deflationary policies and the Murdoch press controlled a formidable chorus, in at least four Australian States at that time: Victoria, South Australia, Queensland and Western Australia. It was a monopoly voice in two of them - South Australia and Western Australia, although there were some separatist murmurings.

Newspaper deliveries by motor vehicles started in January 1936. Soon they were a familiar sight in Flinders Street. (Herald and Weekly Times)

He was at the crest of his vigour as a newspaper controller and as an editor when he threw his support behind Joseph Lyons' fight against the Scullin Labor Government. Writer C.E. Sayers, who knew Murdoch well, said: 'He loved (the fight), caressed every moment of its excitement; wooed the adherents of the things he believed in; detested the men who opposed those things. He may have felt that he was a king-maker, that he was the originator of the policies that were making that king, the conqueror of his opponents.

'But that, of course, was not so. For the first time he was the controller of a massive newspaper campaign; at last he was feeling the power that control of the machine operating that campaign gave. It was a bonny fight and he planned it as such, and saw it as such, using every weapon of pen and printer's ink. The result was never in doubt: everyone knew that. Every dice that was thrown was loaded against Labor. The most successful dice-thrower was J.A. Lyons: the newspapers whether on the sidelines or in the thick of the fight, were his claquers, but Lyons made the fight and won it.'

There is no doubt that Lyons and Murdoch were close in those years; little doubt that Lyons appreciated the support of Murdoch's papers. But there is no evidence that he promised anything for that support. They met often in the months of preparation for the campaign to bring Lyons to the leadership of the Nationalist party and of the campaign that led to the election at which Scullin was inevitably defeated. Murdoch was in the confidence of Lyons as those plans were evolved and there is little doubt that Lyons looked for Murdoch's approval of them. But there is nothing to suggest anything sinister in those frequent contacts, or in the confidences enjoyed between Lyons the prospective Prime Minister and Murdoch the newspaper editor and controller. Most of these meetings took place in the *Herald* office, at luncheons, to which Lyons went in at the front door in full view.

When Lyons announced that he was walking down the steep hill from the Oriental hotel in Collins-st. to the *Herald* office to see Murdoch, a private secretary asked: 'Why don't you get him to see you here: you are the Prime Minister?' Lyons answered: 'Oh, I like Murdoch. It pleases him to see me in his office, and it does me no harm to go there.'

But Murdoch soon became disenchanted with his friend who had grown tired and ill. Before Joe Lyons died, Murdoch was casting about in his mind for a successor. He said in a letter written on 4 January 1939 to his friend Clive Baillieu, who was then in London.

> The picture as I see it is disturbing. On a long view this country has immense changes to make if it is to hold its place amongst white nations. We cannot expect Great Britain to be able to maintain the sea power in both hemispheres necessary for the protection of the whole Empire. But the likelihood of Australian changes being made for the distant danger can be estimated by the waste and inefficiency with which the immediate dangers are being confronted. I therefore take a very grave view of the future and think that almost revolutionary measures must be taken in this country. In this thought I am fully supported by men like Casey, Menzies and Essington Lewis and the leading army officers. But, alas, there is no action in sight. The present position is that Lyons and his wife are quite determined to remain in office. I do not think it would require a long continued demonstration to convince Lyons that he should get out, but he definitely wants to stay in. He has lost his usefulness; he is a conciliator, a peace-man and, of course, a born rail-sitter. Most of the Victorian and South Australian members are hostile to him. The

New South Wales men, however, feel that he is their only electoral asset at the moment. They would, I think, be satisfied with Stevens as the Federal leader for New South Wales and on that condition would accept Menzies as Prime Minister. In November this appeared likely. But Bob has a curiously disconcerting way of discouraging adherence, whilst in fact eagerly seeking it. He is a most difficult man to work for. I do not know whether it is utter laziness or pride. Certainly he is confiding when one is alongside of him, but he never invites confidence. The public is beginning to actually dislike him, which is a great pity. Each week now he is becoming less likely as Prime Minister.

I do not know what we can get out of Lyons, but his wife is an ardent pacifist, even a belligerent pacifist. When he speaks, she speaks; when he gives a Christmas message she gives one. When he appears at the microphone she wants to appear also - and she does. Her message always is that if we love our neighbours enough there will be no war. It is very pitiful and our country is in sore trouble about it.

We should be assuring Britain of support if war comes; Lyons specifically refuses to do it. We should be taking our share of Singapore defence; Lyons will not have it. We should be building a battleship, but Lyons will not do so. We should be forcing new industries and forcing land development to the utmost of its capacity; Lyons sits still. We should have compulsory military service, even if it is only for the national outlook it brings; Lyons is adamant against it. All this because of alleged political impracticabilities. The party will be badly whipped if Hitler does not intervene before the next elections. The party believes that Lyons is its best card - so he is, electorally, if there were no policies at stake.

But even Lyons cannot hold Australia today. The people are tired of the weakness of his Government. Unfortunately they had compulsory insurance badly introduced to them and are against it, and they want a change. Menzies could not stop this drift if he had charge at present, but I feel that big events will change this before the elections come. We all remain on very cordial terms with Lyons, but there is a great deal of disgust being bred.

The United Australia party had made overtures to Labor during 1939 to join an all-party government. The party, led by John Curtin, rejected these overtures, which Murdoch had ardently supported. An all-party war government was to become a major newspaper policy of his throughout the war of 1939-45. Its full impact was to be lost after the Labor party overwhelmingly won the general elections of 1943 and thereafter governed solely because of its majorities in both houses of Parliament.

Murdoch had no doubt about the part Australia should play in the war and he hammered the theme out in his newspapers to make people aware of the gravity of the situation. The step that he took to better inform the public resulted in the major mistake of his career as reporter, publicist and newspaper publisher.

He was appointed Director-General of Information by the wartime Menzies government. A Department of Information had been created whose mission, Menzies said, would be 'to assemble and distribute over the widest possible field and by every available agency the truth about the cause for which we are fighting in this war, information bearing on all phases of the struggle and by its many agencies to keep the minds of the people enlightened as possible and their spirit firm'.

Menzies had told the war cabinet in May 1940: 'The morale of the people is going to undergo a terrific strain and regardless of everything else we should get the best publicists and journalists in Australia to ensure that the press and the people are caught up into the national effort.'

War cabinet authorised him to ask Sir Keith Murdoch if he would undertake the

The shortage of fuel during the Second World War did not prevent the Herald *from being delivered. Horse-drawn vans were used for the first time on 21 October 1942. (Herald and Weekly Times)*

responsibility of making the department effective. Murdoch agreed, if the newspaper industry approved. That approval was obtained and he was formally appointed Director-General of Information on 8 June 1940. He made as a condition of accepting the appointment that he be responsible direct to the Prime Minister and have access to the war cabinet.

The appointment was honorary; he severed all active connection with his newspapers and the industry excepting the newsprint mills in Tasmania, which the Government considered constructive national work, the mills being about to begin production.

Murdoch had fully consulted all city, provincial and country editors throughout Australia before he accepted the Prime Minister's invitation to become Director-General of the Department of Information. Their support and good wishes were unanimous.

As he became involved in what he called 'the affrighting' scope of his duties, Murdoch grew worried about what he would do if a newspaper deliberately published a news item that was false and harmful to Australia's war effort. He had a conference with newspaper editors and controllers on 1 July 1940 to discuss this. He wished to have, he told them, their approval to be able to *compel* a newspaper to correct a mis-statement. 'In certain circumstances the Government should have the right to say that a published statement had been harmful, and to say also, "Here is the truth, print, and print it where we tell you."'

There was immediate protest: this it was said, if carried out, would be a denial of freedom of the press, for which all of them had fought. The censorship, which was within the administration of the Department of Information surely gave the Director-General sufficient power to suppress mis-statement? The power now sought was too wide, and too dangerous. It had within it the germ of dictatorship.

But Murdoch had already talked with the Prime Minister and with the war cabinet about such a regulation allowing him power to use the columns of a newspaper to correct mis-statements. The Prime Minister had agreed with his views. The war cabinet had accepted this, and cabinet approved a regulation to give this power; all the reasons put forward had satisfied it that such power was vital. It was gazetted, and thus was promulgated a blanket power to one man which made him the effectual controller of the press, radio and all other media of publicity in Australia. It was a *gaffe*, the greatest in Keith Murdoch's professional life; it was a thunder-bolt that made him a failure as Director-General of Information; it was a negation of all the things upon which he had built his life as a newspaper man.

What caused it?

Paul Hasluck wrote:

> Inasmuch as the War Cabinet minutes record that 'The views of the Director-General generally were approved by War Cabinet', the responsibility for this policy was accepted by Cabinet. The same point had been discussed by Murdoch with Menzies two days earlier and the Prime Minister was reported to have been in agreement that it was desirable for the Government to obtain this authority.
>
> To appreciate the reasons behind the decision of Cabinet it is necessary to recall the circumstances in which they found themselves after the fall of France, at a moment of great peril to the British Isles and to the British Commonwealth. In the first place they had heard for some weeks past, particularly from the press, a demand for leadership, a demand to tell the people the truth and a demand for an active information policy.
>
> In the second place during the first six months of the war they had encountered many indications of apathy in some sections of the populace and of unwillingness to make a total war effort and they now faced the possibility of an emergency which might require exceptional efforts by the nation.
>
> In the third place the development of that same emergency might present various occasions on which it would be necessary for the Government to make urgent and simultaneous announcements to the people, both by press and radio. They had the powers of censorship, but even when used in the most extreme fashion, this gave only the negative effect of suppression and by itself would probably add to the doubts and uncertainties which were interfering with the national war effort. They had experience, too, of the fact that they could never overtake a rumour.*

Hasluck went on to say that having got approval of his views, Murdoch 'went ahead enthusiastically to translate the new policy into a regulation. But in doing so he was curiously blind to the possible objections of interference with the freedom of the press and apparently did not stop to consider other ways of serving his end, although in the course of drafting some of the dangers were pointed out to him'.

---

*Paul Hasluck, *The Government and the People 1939-41, 1942-5* (Australia in the War of 1939-1945, ser. 4, vols. 1-2) (Canberra, 1952, 1971).

Murdoch claimed that the power to command the use of newspaper space was needed in the national interest, said Hasluck, just as manpower was needed in the armed services and in industry.

The newspapers thought not. The *Sydney Morning Herald* said the regulation 'gives the Department of Information virtual dictatorship'. The Sydney *Daily Telegraph* said: 'The Commonwealth can force you to read statements or opinions which your papers passionately disagree with or believe to be incorrect.' The Sydney *Sun* said: 'The regulation is a crime against the very ideals of freedom for which Australia entered the War.' The Melbourne *Age* said: 'The regulation is objectionable and a dangerous and unnecessary attack on the liberty of the Press and public.'

The only newspapers which did not condemn the regulation were the Melbourne *Herald*, the *Sun News-Pictorial*, and the papers outside Melbourne which Murdoch controlled. They supported a statement made by the Director-General of Information that the regulation would be used sparingly.

Theodore Fink, chairman of directors of the Herald and Weekly Times, protested against the attitude of the *Herald* and the *Sun*. He was ill when the regulation was gazetted; he demanded that it be opposed as an attack on the liberty of the press. His demand was ignored, and he called upon directors of the company to support his view. No action was taken, the directorate view being that the editorial content of the paper was the concern of the managing editor. Fink thereupon wrote a letter which vehemently denounced the regulation 'as an infringement of the rights and liberties of the public'. He dissociated himself from the views expressed in the *Herald's* publications 'in favour of the regulation'. His letter was published in all the leading Australian newspapers, but not in the *Herald*, the *Sun* or the papers in Adelaide and Brisbane.

Murdoch was stung by the criticisms and he was hurt. He said that neither the press nor the radio need have the slightest fear of harm being done them by the use of the powers that the Department of Information might possess. 'If I had sought to be suppressive, or as appears to be mistakenly thought, coercive, I would not have asked for the power to correct persistently damaging statements. I would have been satisfied to use the ample powers that exist of suppressing publication by censorship. I felt and I am convinced it is the right view that suppression by censorship should be avoided where possible and that the best answer to persistent mis-statement is the power to correct it adequately. That is all that the new regulation is intended to mean.'

All disliked the power of suppression, he said, and it was being used to the lightest possible degree. But some forms of lies might be chased promptly and be destroyed by truth. 'They are destructive to the vital war effort, and must be answered. Instead of using suppressive power on such occasions when we cannot get a proper correction of a mis-statement we will be able to use expressive powers. It means nothing more than that.'

This was all very well, said his critics, high-minded, and to be commended as an ideal; but was the Director-General alone to be the judge of the destructiveness of a statement or the strength of a lie?

The regulation was withdrawn, a watered-down version took its place; it was never acted upon. It provided the Director-General with the power to require publication of his own matter when he thought it expedient in the interests of defence or the prosecution of the war, but only in the case of mis-statement or misrepresentation of facts. But first he must furnish the statement to the newspaper concerned and request its publication. If the request was not complied with, he might with approval of the minister, require that the statement be published in such form as he specified. But he could not direct what space it should occupy, but only that it should have a corresponding position and equal prominence.

Murdoch's miscalculation ruined any chance he may have had of succeeding in the wartime information job.

The Prime Minister announced on 14 November 1940: 'The work of the Department of Information is now well established and Sir Keith Murdoch feels that he could in future make a more effective contribution to the strengthening of public opinion and the winning of the war by resuming active association with his newspaper interests.'

Back behind his large antique desk on the third floor at the *Herald* Murdoch picked up the cudgels again to do battle with his old enemy Prime Minister Curtin ... to tell Britain Australia was with her through thick and thin ... to thank the United States for her great help. He took off on a world trip and once or twice fell foul of the censors. In April 1943 he complained under his own by-line from London: 'We have too much complacency and too much censorship; the latter feeds the former. We have too much politics in high places and too many political propagandists; the latter feed on Government pay or Government favours, but their use is politics. We have too much exaggeration in public statements, alternating between triumph and threat.' His piece was 'spiked'. The censor prohibited its publication in the public interest.

On occasion he was clumsily unfair to public leaders, as when he suggested that John Curtin had urged non-conscription in the war of 1914-18 so that he could avoid Army service, whereas in fact Curtin was declared medically unfit for the Army; and when he said John Dedman, a member of Curtin's ministry, did very little in the 1914-18 war, whereas he was in fact an officer in a British regiment.

He became fiercely embroiled in politics, but as the war years passed he was doing some personal re-assessment. Australia had to find a clearer position and a clearer duty, he was saying in September 1943. Faith in individualism had to be reborn, nourished, given stature and purpose. He saw the beliefs of the Labor Party as being: that the waste and pain of unemployment should not recur; a greater Australia required better-educated, better-cared-for and better-paid people, in many cases better housed, in some cases better born; capacity and character must be found and brought forth wherever they exist, irrespective of money.

Murdoch saw little fault in these Labor beliefs, in fact he found a sneaking regard for some of them. He had been personally wounded by the ballot box when he thought he could have forced the Labor Party out of office. Now he believed, he said, that 'the Depression was necessary to teach us that new social and money controls are necessary and possible; the war has given us the grace and proved the national necessity to apply them; we inevitably move into a third phase - that of applying new knowledge'.

This was a high point of his political idealism. But he wavered at that point, found himself concerned 'where the line is to be drawn between the State control of the nation's economy and the individual's necessity for freedom to develop himself and his family ...'

Murdoch's mention of 'family' was significant, for this was never far from his mind ...

On a balmy summer's day at Cruden Farm Sir Keith's guests who had just come in from a gallop along the leafy lanes would be offered a choice of Rhine wine or barley water. It was part of the Murdoch style, just as carefully English as the well-cut tweed jacket Murdoch wore, the jodphurs and the polished riding boots. Miss Kimpton, who was the Murdoch children's governess for eighteen years, says: 'I believe he enjoyed the title. He got great pleasure from it all. And why not?'

Particular pleasure came too from an 'all-dayer' picnic at Point Leo where Murdoch could settle down in a deckchair with his hat over his eyes hoping not to be bothered, unless it was to go fishing in a dinghy with his children or for a ride along the back roads of Baxter with the family and friends. 'It was like a medieval cavalcade,' recalls author Joan Lindsay, 'with children, outriders, horses and dogs; at the head of the procession: Sir Keith mounted on a massive charger, an upright, rather heavily built figure . . . proud and happy in the company of his lively and affectionate brood.' Beside him rode Elisabeth, 'slim and fearless', on a half-wild racehorse that was liable to bolt the last few miles home to the stables. Guests and children would be mounted on a motley collection of steeds ranging from handsome ex-police horses to shaggy little ponies. 'Poor Basil Burdett (Sir Keith's art adviser and the only man heard in the office to call him 'Keith'), hating and fearing all horses, would jog his unhappy way on a solid little pony, his long legs almost touching the ground.'

Riders would return to the farm for Sunday lunch, a good roast beef and a fine claret to wash it down; showers would be taken before lunch and clothes changed. It was a rule that nobody sat down to a meal in riding gear. The horses would have been stabled by then in fine stables that had been built by out-of-work locals during

Keith Murdoch owned a collection of horses from handsome ex-police horses to shaggy ponies. Here he is in the stable yard with baby Helen and Anne (right) and one of his favourite dogs, 'Radiant Ruby of Erindale'.

the Depression; and Cruden farmhouse had been transformed into a commodious country house in the American colonial style, with Georgian porticos and big, open fireplaces. The toilet had arms like an armchair, a basket-weave lid and a flushing lever that was not unlike that on a hand-operated petrol bowser.

Outside Sir Keith had put in sunken gardens, tennis courts, rockeries and an avenue of eucalypts lining the driveway to the road. A loyal gardener who would work 16 hours a day unless he was dissuaded, planted flowers and erected fences to Sir Keith's instructions. 'But Keith had no practical idea of gardening,' said Dame Elisabeth, 'and therefore no conception of how long it should take to accomplish a task. He would be surprised that a fence hadn't gone up the day after he had ordered it.'

Perhaps because he had married late in life, Murdoch was more intense in his enjoyment of his four children: Helen, born in 1929, Rupert in 1931, Anne in 1935 and Janet in 1939. He was a little more aware than a younger father might have been of their *preciousness*; realising that had he not married when he did, they might not have been with him. Governess Miss Kimpton ('Kimpo') noticed that now and again he stretched their energies a little too much, unaware of their limited endurance of a heavy ride, an all-day picnic, a rather formal meeting with guests. He liked to play with them in the evening and would be put out if the governess came to pack them off to bed. 'Oh, Kimpo, just a little while longer . . .'

'He was a strong man, and after riding with them all day, he would be rather surprised that they couldn't go on for quite so long as he did.'

When they were invited out to friends' homes for parties or a meal Sir Keith would give his permission, 'but he would be a little sad that they had gone. He would have liked them to stay home with him'.

Murdoch was strict about his children's politeness to servants. 'You must always be kind to people,' he would tell them. 'Once Rupert was a little rude,' said Miss Kimpton, 'Sir Keith was terribly put out about it.' As punishment, his father took away Rupert's roller skates for a day or two.

Rupert at home could not bear any dissension, said Dame Elisabeth. 'He was a very gentle little boy.'

Wherever he was, Keith Murdoch's thoughts were never far from his family. He confided in a letter to his 10-year-old daughter Anne, from New York, that the city was terribly expensive. 'You'll have to get a good husband to bring you here, because I don't think I will ever be able to afford to bring all my family to this place of monstrous prices unless I can strike it rich!' Later, from his London hotel: 'My most beautiful, roly-poly and sugar custard Anne . . . the weather is foul. I have had to put on my thick undies. I have a drawer full of my lighter summer unmentionables and have not worn any of them . . . All my love darling, and two atomic bombs of kisses and hugs. Your adoring Daddy.'

While Sir Keith worked after dinner in the library on his business papers he seemed unconcerned that the children were scampering noisily playing games almost under his feet. He had the ability to single-mindedly concentrate on what he was doing.

If he took time from his papers and business documents to read for pleasure, it was from a wide selection of political biographies, fly-fishing books, art tomes or modern poetry, which he would occasionally read out to share with the family.

10 'What time's Evensong?'

In 1943 there was what observers have called an audacious move by Dr H.V. Evatt, the Minister for External Affairs, to entice Murdoch away from his vociferous newspapers and into 'public life'. Evatt quietly asked a senior *Herald* man to make an 'unofficial' sounding on Murdoch's attitude to a posting as a high commissioner in one of the Dominions, or as a Minister-at-Large in South America with headquarters probably in Chile. Murdoch was amused, and he told his staff man, 'Tell your friend that I must continue to work for national government.'

All his life he had been embroiled in politics, first as a reporter of the political arena and latterly as a proprietor whose considerable voice was listened to and courted. Might he ever consider going into politics himself? his friends sometimes wondered.

Harold Cox, his Canberra bureau chief, says, 'He asked me once, what I thought about it, and I said quite frankly that I thought he'd be very unhappy in Parliament. He would only have been a target for the Labor Party which was always referring to the 'Murdoch Octopus'. If he got into Parliament he'd have really copped it from them.'

Frederick Howard, his leader writer, is certain that he did once seriously consider entering politics just after the war. 'He discussed it with Ralph Simmonds, who edited the *Herald* for so many years, and Ralph told me about it, just before he died.

'Sir Keith said to Ralph: "I've been approached and it has been suggested that I might go into Federal politics. What do you think, Ralph?"

'Simmonds said: "I don't think it would be a good idea, K.M."

"Why not?" asked Sir Keith.

"Well," said Simmonds, "I don't think you're well-enough known to the ordinary man in the street. I think you're a little remote from the ordinary people - you wouldn't be very successful."

"Ahh. Remote, you think," smiled Murdoch. "Hmmm. Maybe you're right. I'll tell you what, Ralph. Today we won't lunch at the Melbourne Club, we'll go down to the Athenaeum." '

'I think he *played* with the idea of politics,' said Dame Elisabeth, 'but I don't think he had the confidence in himself to take the final step. I think it would have been disastrous had he done so, because he was far too sensitive a man. I think he honestly believed that what he had to give, he could give better through journalism.'

On a sleepy Melbourne Saturday midday in August 1947, when citizens were getting ready to go to the football, the Chifley Government dropped a bombshell. After a cabinet meeting, Ben Chifley, the pipe-puffing, former engine-driver, almost casually announced: 'Cabinet today authorised the Attorney-General (Dr H.V. Evatt) and myself to prepare legislation for submission to the Federal Parliamentary Labor party for the nationalisation of banking, other than State banks, with proper protection for the share-holders, depositors, borrowers and staffs of private banks.'

Murdoch was electrified. He saw the attack on the banks as a chance at last for the slowly emerging new Liberal party with its toughened leader, R.G. Menzies, to bundle Chifley out of office. His papers immediately demanded a referendum which Chifley rejected; a referendum could deal only with the Bill's constitutionality.

The legislation was given the Royal assent in November 1947. An appeal was made to the High Court on the constitutional aspect. The Court decided against the legislation. The Government appealed to the Privy Council. That hearing lasted from 14 March to 1 June 1949. The Judicial Committee rejected the appeal, thus voiding the Act.

The Chifley government went before the people at a general election on 10 December 1949. It was defeated, and the new Liberal party came into office with ministers from the Country party. Murdoch's hopes for a reborn Liberalism were realised.

As a newspaper controller and editor, occupied with the barometer of political thrust, Murdoch had to find time almost daily to meet and discuss important issues with im-portant men. Frustratingly, he often found himself shackled without warning by his old stammer; he was again on the other side of that 'wall'. It occurred particularly at times of heavy stress or when he spoke in public. Political leaders who waited on him to persuade him of their point of view would sometimes come away worried that they had not conveyed their message adequately; he had seemed preoccupied.

Douglas Brass, one of Murdoch's special correspondents who was close to him, noticed that although his mind was fertile and active and packed with all sorts of ideas – most of them progressive ones – he found difficulty communicating them to other people. His shyness was a perplexing thing to understand. 'I was with him in talks with senior British ministers and generals, and there was this diffidence of manner in conversation, even though it had determination behind it. He wanted to find out about things and to interpret them; to pump people. All of this must have been a strain on a man of such superficial nervousness.

'It gave me the impression when I first met him that he wasn't interested in what we were discussing. Later I was to find that was a wrong impression. He was *always* keen to understand people, to assess, to discover what they were thinking; and above all, to discover what they knew. Murdoch was basically a reporter ...'

He could behave as one three or four times a week when he sat at the head of the table in the board room dining-room with guests gathered from every walk of public life. To these affairs were invited men and women of substance who had some-thing to contribute. They enjoyed good food, fine clarets, Rhine wines and Havana cigars. Sir Keith might join them by taking a whisky, first with soda, but latterly with water, before lunch, or ordering a gin and bitters, first swirling the bitters around in his glass and then tossing it into a receptacle (or sometimes missing and hitting the carpet), then allowing his gin to be poured. He would take a glass of white wine, but rarely a second one.

His purpose in gathering people about him was to question, probe, grill, and cross-examine them. He wanted to know what was going on – in business, politics, inter-national diplomacy, art, medicine. 'He pumped and he pumped,' said a former staffer

In August 1947 Ben Chifley announced his proposal to nationalise Australian banks. After a series of appeals the legislation was rejected. Here a crowd gathers outside the Bank of New South Wales after the High Court invalidated the legislation. Murdoch bitterly opposed the plan.

who attended many lunches. 'And strangely there was never any sign of his stammer while he was being the reporter. It only appeared when he was making a formal speech, or afterwards if you saw him in his office alone and told him your wife was dying and asked if he could help.'

Sir Keith was told confidences at these luncheons and at his own dinner table, and he would have dearly loved to print many. But he did not. What was discussed on such occasions, he assured his guests, was not for his newspapers.

When, on the other hand, he was probing people 'on the record' he did it expertly and communicated the results succinctly to whatever newsman or department was going to handle it. Lyle Turnbull, editor-in-chief of the *Herald* and the *Sun*, says: 'He was constantly seeking information, sifting it, analysing it. This large, bulky, impressive man who was a curious blend of shyness and strength was an expert communicator. I went once on a short visit to Taiwan and he got me into the little file room at the *Herald's* office in London and asked me: "What do you think about China?" ... a rather large question to ask a 22-year-old who had spent just three days in Taipei.

'I was going through an old desk he must have used at some stage and in one of the drawers was his itinerary for a trip he'd made to America in the late forties. He was there for two weeks and almost every hour of those two weeks he'd had an appointment arranged before he'd even left Melbourne. He saw the President, the Secretary of State, people in the publishing world; he gave speeches and saw everybody of any importance at all.'

Murdoch was re-examining every section of the *Herald* to make it more readable, informative and comprehensive. He had familiarised himself with all kinds of sport (grudgingly admitting that space should be given to racehorse tipping), finance, world affairs, politics, gardening and art. Now he found himself tip-toeing carefully through the potentially explosive minefield of the women's pages. 'In the early forties,' recalls Pat Jarrett, one of his best women's editors, 'the women's pages had been called "the social pages" and they consisted of stereotyped reports of social gatherings. These were described and located in the first paragraph, and then followed columns of names and initials under the line: "Among those present were ..." '

Murdoch had appointed Miss May Maxwell as his first women's editor and provided her with a private bathroom (equipped with bath), toilet, and a key ensuring that it would be for her personal use only. Pat Jarrett, who then worked on the general reporting staff, said: 'The women's section was known rather derogatorily then as "The Butterfly Department". Reporters on the social pages had to recognise a social figure, and get her initials right.'

After serving as a war correspondent and reporting the American scene for the *Herald*, Pat Jarrett returned to be informed by the then *Sun* editor, Jack Waters, that Sir Keith wanted her as the new women's editor. *She was appalled.* 'You can't do that to me! Not the Butterfly Department!'

Waters replied: 'You once told me the social pages should be about what women did, rather than what they wore. Go and tell "K.M." what you think.

'So I was called in. I said to Sir Keith: "We will really have to change things if I take the job. I don't think we have any room for social *piddle* any more." He was shocked. He reached into his drawer and pulled out a bunch of gum-leaves which he proceeded to wave under his nose. I had polluted the air!'

When the war came to an end Murdoch Men who had served as war correspondents or fought overseas began gradually returning to Flinders-st. to the parish-pump parochialism in which the threatened slaughter of a tree in St Kilda-rd. called out the services of two reporters and a photographer.

A newcomer to the reporters' room was John Blanch, an ex-major who had been one of the last to leave Singapore before it fell to the Japanese. Blanch had encountered

Sir Keith Murdoch at a Melbourne luncheon just before the end of the war and had dared to criticise his outspoken views on the defence of Singapore. Surprised at the contradiction, Murdoch had asked him to lunch, been impressed by the young officer and had then written to him in the Solomon Islands offering him a job after the war. Blanch accepted and found himself not so much occupied with heavy decisions like outwitting the enemy, but rather, making sure he did not miss his cadet shorthand classes.

'Typical of Sir Keith's efforts to see what you were made of would be to call you in and say, as he said to me: "Ah ... Blanch. I have decided to give a luncheon at the Windsor Hotel next Tuesday week for forty people. Would you be so kind as to organise it, arrange the menu, the seating, the budget, etc.?" Or ... "Blanch. I am going to Brisbane tomorrow to attend the board of Queensland Newspapers. Would you accompany me and go over the annual report?" '

When John Blanch became the Herald and Weekly Times London business manager, he and the London editor, Trevor Smith, worked for days before each impending arrival of 'K.M.', to prepare answers to every possible question in every possible field. 'We tested one another on the way down to the airport in the hired Daimler, with Trevor playing Sir Keith, and me playing me.'

Sir Keith stepped, beaming, off the aircraft on one trip. 'Good morning boys! What time's Evensong at St Paul's?'

Herald men, now greying or bald, recall their sudden summons in those days of the forties to Miss Demello's office and an 'invitation' to dine at the Murdoch home the following evening. Frantic phone calls would be made to wives who in turn made pleading calls to hairdressers, reminding their husbands to buy a new shirt before Ball & Welch closed at 5.30 pm. 'One was absolutely terrified of using the wrong knife or fork,' said *Sun* Foreign Affairs commentator, Douglas Wilkie. 'You were met at the door by a uniformed butler and waited upon at the table by servants. You had to pretend not to be over-awed by the plate, the glassware and the antique silver and to endeavour to comment knowledgeably on the wine.'

Attempting to draw a young couple into the conversation on one such danger-fraught occasion, Sir Keith inquired of the cadet reporter's wife: 'Do you like old things, my dear?'

'Oh yes,' she blushed. 'I am very fond of you, Sir Keith.' 'Whereupon,' recalled the witness to the occasion, 'Lady Murdoch choked on her soup.'

When Keith Dunstan, in later years to become a columnist for the *Sun*, was invited to the Murdoch table he was warned by his father, Bill Dunstan, general manager of the Herald and Weekly Times and Murdoch's right-hand man for thirty years, 'Make sure you're out of the house by 10 o'clock. Sir Keith won't want you there any later than that.' Dunstan senior, a VC, had a 'curious love-hate relationship' with Sir Keith, said his son. 'He was often in despair over his expenditure on works of art for his office or the board room, or over some dispute about the rationed newsprint allocation. Father would come home and say "that terrible man". Yet woe betide you if you agreed with him. If you ever said anything critical about Sir Keith he would get very angry indeed and say: "How dare you talk about him like that - he's one of the greatest men in the country."

'I went off in some trepidation to dine at the Toorak house, and joined one or two other cadets around the dinner table. We were trying to make small-talk, with the butler waiting on us, and Sir Keith up at the top of the table carving the chicken, which was a luxury in those days. This bird appeared to be a little resilient, and all of a sudden, when he made a hard thrust downwards with the knife to try and sever a leg, the chicken skidded off the plate across the table and landed on the floor. There was a stunned silence while Sir Keith hesitated for a moment; then he reached down, picked it up and started carving it again. He never said a word about the incident. Dad was also right about the time to depart. After brandies we were being taken on the grand tour of the paintings and Georgian silver when I glanced at my watch to make sure it wasn't yet 10 o'clock. Sir Keith strode over to me and said: "Well, Keith, I suppose you'll be needing your coat." And a manservant went off and got it.'

Sir Keith usually carved with dexterity and some aplomb, but other practical activities like changing a fuse or hanging a picture were beyond his capabilities. He had little idea about the mechanics of things, and his knowledge of cars and the internal combustion engine would not have filled many lines of his newspaper. (He was, in short, a danger to drive with.) 'We landed at Brisbane airport one afternoon,' says John Blanch, 'to be met by a chauffeur-driven limousine which was obviously running quite roughly. Sir Keith noticed it and asked me what I thought might be wrong. I said: "It sounds like a blown gasket to me." Whereupon "K.M." leaned forward, opened the glass sliding partition and announced to the driver: "*Ted, you have blown a gaskin.*" '

At the wheel himself he tended to have his mind on more important affairs than propelling the vehicle. 'He enjoyed *the idea* of driving,' said Dame Elisabeth, 'but he would not concentrate on the job. On the way down to Cruden Farm one day, he went right through the red lights at a road junction. The police happened to be there and they pulled him up. They were very nice and understanding and sent him on his way with a warning. On the way back to Melbourne he came to the junction

and did exactly the same thing! The same police were still there and they flagged him down. When they saw it was him they just said: "You're hopeless." '

If fine art, rare antiques and good silver were perhaps uppermost among Murdoch's acquisitive desires, close behind was his fascination for gadgetry - particularly the latest in fountain pens. 'If you had a new pen, Sir Keith would stop by your desk and rather pointedly admire it,' says Douglas Brass. 'His admiration would be so great that you would say: "I wonder if you would like to have it, Sir Keith?" And he would "hesitatingly" accept it.'

'The top, left-hand drawer of his desk,' says Herald and Weekly Times chairman, Keith Macpherson, who sits behind it now, 'was full of pens. I should know, because as a lad on the *Herald* it was my job to clean and fill them. In the late 1930s the first Parker pens came out and you were supposed to fill them with a special ink, called "Quink". Sir Keith used to fill his with rather cheaper school ink and of course they clogged up and wouldn't work. I would collect them and take them to the washroom where I would squirt them out and then re-fill them with Quink. I would never dare tell him to fill them with the dearer ink, but I would tell Miss Demello ... Sir Keith would go on collecting pens, but even then he didn't use them much, he preferred a wooden-handled pen with a broad "Jay" nib and we used to buy them for him in packets of six. The "Jay" nibs accounted for his rather broad signature.'

The same pens sometimes snagged when Sir Keith was signing cheques, causing a large blot over the Murdoch signature. He would call in his secretary and hand her the cheque, torn from the cheque-book. 'Ah, Miss Demello. It appears I have spoiled this cheque. Would you be so kind as to drop it into the bank next time you're passing? We can then get credit for the duty stamp.'

That night, the man who could be so tough about employees' incomes, might go home and have to be called to the front door by the butler confronting somebody in trouble. 'Once a woman came to the door and said she was dying. She said she was worried that she might not have enough to pay for her funeral,' recalls the family governess. 'Sir Keith had never met the woman and knew nothing about her. But he gave her the money.'

Rohan Rivett, who worked for him as a reporter and later became a renowned author, remembered a young Tasmanian arriving to see Sir Keith about a job. 'There were the usual pauses between the young reporter being dreadfully shy with the big chief, and "K.M." being always shy with the young reporter. "K.M." finally pressed him to a cup of tea. Embarrassed, the reporter accepted gratefully. "K.M.", without looking, poured tea into the only cup available which had already been used by a member of the board. After all the fuss, the reporter forgot to drink it. The upshot of it was that "K.M." lent him £78 to keep him going while he looked for a job.'

'He never knew what any of us felt about him,' said a reporter who did get a job. 'He would have been too modest to let himself believe it.'

Sir Keith with Sir Winston Churchill leaving a session of the Empire Press Conference in 1946. Murdoch's post-war years were filled with many busy and demanding trips overseas.

11 Borrowed time

Keith Murdoch's immediate friends, his family and top executives of the *Herald*, knew that at the end of the 1940s 'K.M.' was living on borrowed time. Which would give in first - the stubborn, workaholic Murdoch or his heart? At the end of 1949 Murdoch reluctantly called in Miss Demello, and said he wished to dictate a message.

It was to be his Christmas message to the whole organisation he headed, *and his farewell*. 'I am handing over to others many of my duties that have kept me in such close contact with all your affairs. I am near the company's official retiring age ... I have four other compulsions on me. They are from my wife, my doctors, my conscience and my commonsense. An irresistible team.'

He would resign as managing director of the Herald and Weekly Times, and retire from the directorate of Advertiser Newspapers Ltd., Adelaide. He was 64, and since the early 1930s when he had a severe breakdown caused by heart strain, he had never been well. He had been an incessant, tireless worker all his life and he had one failing that prevented him from putting back into his system what he was taking out of it: he could not relax. Elisabeth tried to take him on holidays, but it was no use. Sir Keith would annually take part in the charade about 'what a really lovely holiday we are going to have somewhere ...' 'We were *really* going to have a fortnight off this time,' said Dame Elisabeth. 'We would in fact go to the beach or to the country; but at the end of five days there was always some good reason why he had to dash off to Brisbane or Adelaide or back to the office. He could relax superbly for a very short time, but for no longer. There was no way he could sit on the beach and read. We would try; we would take our boat to Davey's Bay which was a lovely place to take the children so they could swim and go fishing; but for Keith to have to go down and sit on the beach was purgatory. He would take a bag of work, settle into a deckchair and pray that nobody would speak to him.'

Murdoch retained the position of chairman of directors of the company and came in every day as though nothing had changed.

He had been told he was over-working. But he had ignored his doctors and their bulletins and the debt to his constitution was piling up.

His recovery from his first heart attack was slow, if he ever fully recovered from it. In a letter to Charles Bean as early as 1934 he said: 'I am supposed to be recovered from my bit of a breakdown. I have had an over-strained heart and it has required a lot of rest. My recovery however has been slow and to complete the cure the doctors are sending me away for three months.' He was about to leave Australia for the ordered three months' recovery rest when he had a second heart attack. He was ill for several months, and altogether he was away from the office for about a year.

In the garden at Cruden Farm in 1932: (standing from left) Miss de Lancey Forth, Mr Rupert Greene, the Reverend P. J. Murdoch, (seated from left) Miss Helen Murdoch, Rupert Murdoch, Keith and Elisabeth Murdoch, Mrs P. J. Murdoch and Mrs de Lancey Forth.

This attack had come after a strenuous game of tennis Murdoch had with Mr Neville Fraser, the present Prime Minister's father, at the Murdoch home in Toorak. 'They played two or three sets and I think Keith rather overdid it,' said Dame Elisabeth. 'It was just at a time when he'd had rather a badly infected tooth out and he just wasn't well.'

Murdoch's doctor gave him a grim report of his heart condition and ordered him to rest for a year. It was a year in the wilderness for the restless newspaperman. Forbidden to go to the office he divided his time between Melbourne and Cruden Farm, disconsolately reading newspapers and books, criticising to anybody who would listen some of the things that were happening to the *Herald*. 'It was a very unhappy time. People were spreading horrid rumours about,' said Dame Elisabeth. 'They were very harmful and they were designed to be. People would come down to Cruden Farm to see him and they would sit out in the garden in the long chairs and tell him what was happening.'

When Murdoch was pronounced fit enough to go to the office he discovered his worst fears were true: there was a plot to get rid of him, to force his retirement from the company, taking away his executive powers. The battle came to a head at a board meeting when Murdoch put forward his views about the future of the paper. He was opposed by Theodore Fink whose camp wanted Fink's son Thorold to replace Murdoch. There was a new board member present - George Caro - and when the vote came Caro sided with Murdoch and the Finks were beaten. Murdoch afterwards always referred to Caro as 'a white man'.

He continued to thrash himself. He faced up to new problems on top of his daily labours: newsprint making, amalgamation of newspapers and of rival cable newsagencies, establishment of Australian Associated Press and the postwar partnership with Reuter, art gallery administration, which in itself could have been a fulltime activity, and the short-lived directorship of the wartime Department of Information.

Few people outside his immediate family and closest newspaper associates knew much about the seriousness of illnesses that he passed through in the last dozen years of his life: years that slowed his reactions, but not his courage or his tenacious endeavour for things that he believed in and fought for.

Apart from the heart attacks, he had been through a complicated prostate-gland operation which at the time was far more serious a surgical undertaking than it is now. Then after a lengthy medical examination at 62, he was informed by his doctors that he had cancer of the bowel; the growth was advanced and would have to be operated on immediately.

The prognosis was, said his wife, 'bad and frightening'. Murdoch was given no bright forecasts that he would even survive the operation and his doctors warned him that if he came through it his future would not be known for ten days after it had taken place.

His surgeons believed that they had removed all the cancerous tissue and they had avoided the necessity of a colostomy, which was at least some relief. But Sir Keith's life was in the balance for the next ten days. He remained in hospital for another six weeks, during which time he sent notes to Miss Demello about tying up business affairs - finding time to send her money to cover her dentist's bill and to urge her to take a week or so off ('but not just yet'). Then he had the all-clear from the doctors and the family breathed a sigh of relief. There were renewed promises to take it easy, to enjoy time off with his family ... the usual pretence of planning a holiday.

From the time he had his first heart attack he also suffered from fibrillations, in which the heart muscle twitches unevenly and the heart can actually stop beating requiring urgent electric stimulation. It happened regularly when he was going through stress.

'I would know what was going to happen the moment he came in from work,' says Dame Elisabeth. 'If he had to dismiss anybody he would be utterly wretched. He would come through the door and I could see he was rather emotional; I knew that almost unfailingly it would bring on one of his attacks. He would spend half the night lying awake trying to force himself to go into the office next day to do what he had to do. And as sure as night follows day, he would have one of his attacks. It was hard for me to watch him and be powerless; knowing he had to go through this turmoil. For he knew he was going to have to hurt somebody and for him it was agony, knowing these people had a home and family to support.' On rare occasions the turmoil he was going through would force him to take to his bed for a day.

Murdoch was understandably anxious about his health. But paradoxically, he was bad about taking medicine. He would forget to take pills prescribed by his doctors and would sometimes drive up to his station outside Canberra with no medication whatsoever. Harold Cox would get a phone call alerting him that Murdoch's heart condition was distressing him and asking Cox to get one of his chief's doctor friends to quickly dispatch some digitalis to Booroomba.

Part of his stress problem was over-work, part because he was bad at delegating responsibility. Heavy blame for the tension he was going through could also be put down to his innate thirst for security which he tried to assuage, on one hand, by working harder and trying to control more investments, and on the other, by having to use borrowed funds to bring about this control. His mind was also constantly occupied with what was happening to the *Herald* when he was away from the office. He felt it was constantly slipping back from the high quality standards he had set for it and he was dissatisfied.

He worried incessantly about his family's future and that they might not have enough money when he died. 'In those days,' said Dame Elisabeth, 'bank overdrafts were much more frightening than they seem to be today; the way people operate on overdrafts terrifies me, and I think it would have terrified Keith. I could not sleep in my bed knowing I owed anybody money.

'Keith was not quite so anxious as that; but he was so respected and trusted that the banks would lend him anything. I think this was wrong. I think they over-did it and Keith was a little embarrassed for a time. He wasn't very well and he'd had a couple of big operations. When he went into hospital to be operated on for cancer he had quite a large overdraft and it disturbed him greatly.'

His son, Rupert, says: 'Looking back now on an overdraft of £70,000 . . . it must have seemed formidable. My father went on trying to build up assets, and was advised not to put all his eggs into one basket, so he put a large proportion of his assets into pastoral properties. At times he was terribly badly advised. He only had about 5 per cent of *Herald* shares, whereas if he had put his money into what he knew about, rather than trying to be a Collins-st. farmer, he would have died a very rich man.

'He enjoyed the office, but he worried about it a lot. He would come home and talk about the agonies of responsibility; of fights he was having at the National Gallery; fights with the Victorian Premier to get land for the gallery; fights to get money for the new building. There were problems in the office regarding old-fashioned religious prejudices. He was suspicious of a Catholic clique being formed and was just as suspicious of the Masons who were sometimes very bigoted and scheming.'

When Murdoch was packed off to hospital for an operation he would take a miniature chess board and a book of chess games with him. 'He liked to work out the moves and use strategy - just like he did in business,' said Dame Elisabeth.

He was in good form when, about a month before the controversial 1950 Bill to outlaw the Communist party was introduced, he flew to Canberra and dined at the Lodge with Prime Minister Menzies. In the course of the meal Menzies gave Murdoch a rough draft outline of what was proposed in the Bill, which would make it a criminal offence to hold Communist ties. Shortly afterwards, Murdoch went on an overseas trip and was on his way home by sea when the Bill was introduced.

'When I saw it I was absolutely horrified by it,' said the *Herald's* man in Canberra of the day, Harold Cox. 'I regarded it as the most violently reactionary measure that had been introduced in a British parliament in two hundred years.

'Jack Williams (later Sir John) was acting for Murdoch while he was away and I told him on the phone what I thought of it. "It's the biggest bitch of a Bill I have ever seen," I said. And I gave him a whole series of reasons why I thought so. Williams said: "Are you prepared to write what you have told me?" '

Cox replied: 'Are you prepared to publish it?'

Cox wrote his article and it was published. The presses in Flinders-st. had hardly stopped spilling out the final edition of the *Herald* when Murdoch's ship docked at Port Melbourne. He was on the phone to Cox early next morning.'Young man, have you taken leave of your senses?' he wanted to know.

'I don't think so, Sir Keith,' replied Cox.

'But that article you had in the paper last night!'

'What's wrong with it, Sir Keith?'

'Oh dreadful, dreadful.'

'Well, I think it's right. And I think in the course of time you'll come to see that.'

'Well, all I've got to tell you is this: if I had been home you would never have got away with that.'

'And that,' said Cox, 'was the end of it. No feelings of hostility. No grudge.'

After the High Court invalidated the proposed legislation the Government held a referendum to change the constitution. It was defeated.

As the newspaper proprietor's mantle settled comfortably about Murdoch's shoulders he had unconsciously developed an air of remoteness that some mistakenly saw as eccentricity. It enabled him to get away with a lot more than people gave him credit for. 'It seemed that he was thinking of something else while you were speaking to him,' said one of his former executives. 'You therefore went into a bit more detail to try and get through to him, heavily emphasising the points you wanted to get across. He would be gazing at the ceiling or out the window to the Jolimont railway yards and then all of a sudden he would throw in a question which showed he was taking in all you had said and you had better have given him the correct fact in the first place because he repeated it to you.'

'... Good morning, Smith,' he would say as he stopped by a desk on one of his forays through the reporters' room. 'What are you on?'

'Oh,' he would muse, as though he hadn't really taken in the answer. Then, 'What are you reading at the moment?' (A hurried racking of brains to serve up some book that might be fitting for a young reporter eager to get on in his craft and learn about the outside world.) 'I see. What are you driving these days ...'

Sometimes his mind actually *was* elsewhere. One morning Sir Keith met one of his lady executives as he made his way between the rows of desks with their screwed-down ashtrays. 'Oh, good morning, Miss Jones. When is your mother coming in to have afternoon tea with me? Haven't seen her for a long time.'

'But Sir Keith ... mother passed away two years ago.'

'No. No. You tell her to come in and have tea ...'

'But Sir Keith ...'

'No, Miss Jones. Haven't seen her for weeks. Tell her to give Miss Demello a ring. Must come in for afternoon tea. Good morning to you.'

'Something soaring, something standing apart in lonely grandeur' - the Australian-American Association, of which Sir Keith Murdoch was the first president, and the Federal Government combined to erect this 258-feet-high monument in Canberra to commemorate the Americans who fought as allies with Australia in the Pacific war. (Canberra Times)

109

After Japan's World War II defeat Sir Keith often expressed his concern that the strong ties that had formed between Australia and the United States as allies should be nurtured and not allowed to slacken. He had been instrumental in forming the Australian American Association and had been its first president from 1940-6. 'Now,' he suggested, 'could we not form a similar group in the United States?' It would stimulate American business and government interest in Australia and would go a long way towards overcoming obstacles to investment, like onerous double taxation laws. The *Herald's* bureau chief in America, Randal Heymanson (later Sir Randal), was president of the Australian Society in New York and he talked it over with Charles Gamble, a director of the Standard Vacuum Oil Company, who had headed the American Red Cross in Australia during the war, and with banker Alick McLean who had been decorated for his wartime work as president of the Australian Society of New York.

In July 1946 Randal Heymanson organised a lunch at the University Club, attended by a group of Americans prominent in banking, business and newspapers, and Sir Keith flew across to address it. His forceful ideas galvanised them into a quick general agreement that an American Australian Association should be established and a working committee went into action. In 1948 the Association was incorporated; its objectives: to provide a forum for political and business leaders of America, Australia and New Zealand, enabling them to meet and exchange views; to serve existing American-Australian and New Zealand business and to encourage new developments in commerce and investment; to report on developments in industry and investment in Australia and New Zealand; to be available to both countries as a consultant and advisory agency on American-Australian trade; and to stimulate cultural intercourse between the two countries with the cooperation of organisations in Australia and New Zealand having similar objectives.

Sir Keith Murdoch was also keen that a monument should be erected in Australia to commemorate the Americans who had fought as allies with Australians in the Pacific War, 'something soaring, something standing apart in lonely grandeur'. In 1954 with money raised by the Australian American Association and added to by the Australian Government, a 258-feet high aluminium shaft surmounted by an American eagle, its wings uplifted in the victory sign, was unveiled in Canberra by Her Majesty Queen Elizabeth II. It now dominates the Australian capital.

12 A bitchy world . . .

'He would awaken at 2 am sometimes, and lie there and worry - and that frightened me,' said Dame Elisabeth. It was generally because he had been backed into a corner and there was no way out of having to face the possibility of sacking an executive or a reporter. Resignation as managing director had taken away little of the load of responsibility he always carried in his mind; he was in the office daily, if not directly making decisions on appointments, spending, or what went into leading articles, he was certainly giving an opinion on them.

If dismissals and threatened competition kept him awake and added to his stress so, paradoxically, did his involvement in one of his greatest loves - art. Sir Keith had become entangled in Melbourne's art world as an administrator and - indirectly - as an arbiter of taste; and the resultant bitchiness and sarcasm brought down on his grizzled head had rather astonished him. Artists and their camp-followers were more influenced by emotion than any politician and the words they used more highly charged with venom. If he met attackers face-to-face he had a favourite ploy to end the confrontation. 'We must have a long talk sometime - but not now.'

It began in a gentle way, with Sir Keith satisfying his growing interest in art by collecting in Australia and abroad for his own walls. Then he became friendly with Dame Nellie Melba, a shrewd collector who had been penning articles for him, and Daryl Lindsay, who was to become his chief art adviser. They encouraged him to buy paintings and prints by unknown, but promising, Australian artists. Lindsay took time to talk to Murdoch about Melbourne's National Gallery and the need to improve it. It was dingy, and haphazardly arranged and was becoming a shelter for tramps on cold winter days and passers-by scuttling in from sudden rain storms. It had been left financially well-off by the bequest of Alfred Felton, a bachelor manufacturing chemist who had been frugal in his ways and had grown rich. But though the Felton Bequest conferred on the gallery on his death in 1904 had already enabled it to buy some great works of art, its Trustees had not always been wisely advised on purchases. Lindsay persuaded Murdoch to use his newspapers to help educate the public on art by publishing skilled criticism of paintings and encouraging the use of galleries for artistic enjoyment.

Murdoch's own collection of paintings, silver, Chinese porcelain and furniture had been gathered over the years on forays abroad. He was becoming so well-known in Bond-st. that he would send John Blanch, his London business manager, to bid *incognito* for him if he particularly liked a painting. (Auctioneers recognising Murdoch tended to pull an imaginary bid or two 'off the wall' if he showed an acquisitive interest.) On Daryl Lindsay's advice, Murdoch hired as art critic a tall, sensitive young man,

Basil Burdett, who had a wide and intelligent knowledge of all forms of art.

Another Lindsay - Lionel - who had written the art notes for the *Herald* in the mid-thirties, persuaded Murdoch to seek an appointment as a trustee of the Public Library, which was later split into four administrative trusts, one of them the National Gallery. Murdoch was appointed to the Board of Trustees in 1933, when the gallery was an unenterprising, uninspiring branch of the Public Service and a dreary, if warm, refuge from the weather for those who had little else to do on a dull afternoon. By 1939, when Murdoch was made chairman of the trustees, the *Herald* was explaining the implications of post-impressionism and giving a belated recognition to painters like Rupert Bunny, James Quinn and George Bell. He was encouraging fellow trustees to think on a grander scale and Daryl Lindsay was packed off to purchase important paintings for Melbourne. The gallery had always wanted a Renoir, and now when Lindsay reported from America that he had the chance of buying 'La Promenade', an outstanding example of Renoir's work, Murdoch was enthusiastic. But the Federal Exchange authorities said no; such a large amount of money could not be sent out of Australia. So Lindsay recommended an alternative Renoir, 'Femme Couchée' - a nude. This time Murdoch was not quite so enthusiastic; his innate prudery put him against the portrayal of naked ladies on canvas. He wrote to Lindsay: 'I am sorry that it is a nude. People do not like to see nudes displayed in public galleries.' The question of purchase came up before the Felton Bequests Committee and Murdoch found an ally. A member remarked: 'Alfred Felton would turn in his grave at the thought of such a picture being acquired from his bequest.' The purchase proposal was rejected.

In 1941 the Felton Bequests Committee bought two of Norman Lindsay's water colours. They were delivered to the trustees and Murdoch, pouting, said, 'I consider Norman Lindsay's water colours as having no artistic merit other than showing a great aptitude for illustration. They are in bad taste, in the main badly constructed and their subject matter ill-chosen. They will have no interest to succeeding generations. The two chosen for our decision have been selected because they contain no repulsive Lindsay nudes, but they are none the better for this. To my mind they are ill-constructed, lack substance and are unworthy of our gallery.'

As he remained in the chair for year after year, he became more deeply involved in making the gallery collection an outstanding one. He worked long hours talking to art experts, interviewing directors, writing letters to other galleries, and becoming a little more dictatorial. It irritated him that some of the trustees did not display enough energy and enthusiasm for the job, and he made enemies. One of these was Robert Dunlop Elliott, an art collector, former senator and fellow newspaper proprietor. Elliott, proprietor of Mildura's *Sunraysia Daily*, had been a trustee since 1928, and almost from the moment Murdoch joined the board table sparks began to fly. 'It seemed to me,' said Daryl Lindsay, 'that R.D. Elliott came to the meetings for the purpose of baiting Murdoch or having a crack at me through the chair. It was a battle of wits - Elliott rude and impassioned - Murdoch slow of speech but polite.'

Murdoch had another antagonist - art-teacher Max Meldrum, a colourful, dogmatic painter who was an *enfant terrible* of the Melbourne art world. 'He had rather a fixed mind on painting,' said Lindsay, 'and could not stomach anything that was not based on tone values, his strong point. He would labour this point, saying: "After all, I am an expert adviser to this Committee." Murdoch would come back with: "Our director is our expert adviser and I think we should respect his opinion, even if it differs from yours, Mr Meldrum."'

112

What had been dull stuff indeed for reporters yawning their way through monthly meetings of the trustees suddenly made good newspaper copy. They watched for Elliott and Murdoch to find a difference of opinion and they were seldom disappointed. The heated exchanges at the meetings were so gleefully served up next day on the news pages that Murdoch, seeking to defend himself from the reportage of his own profession, thought it might be better to hold discussions *in camera*. He wrote to one of the trustees, John Medley, Vice-Chancellor of Melbourne University, about it:

> We had a stormy meeting yesterday. Elliott and Meldrum both being argumentative and vociferous and foolish in front of the Press. I fear it is going to be necessary to meet behind closed doors and give out our news to the Press. We do not want a brawl in public, and these two fellows are determined to do nothing but advertise themselves.

He even sought to by-pass his enemies around the trustees' table and cut pieces out of correspondence they had to see, or failed to give them letters at all. But his 'selective circulation' was discovered by Elliott who wrote to him:

> You mention a wire that you received from Lindsay, but you haven't sent it to the Trustees. I should be glad to receive a copy: also have you circulated the full text of letters from Lindsay? There seem to be some gaps in the ones I have received.

Controversy surrounded Sir Keith in his later years over his involvement in Melbourne's art world. Here, with the artist Russell Drysdale, he looks at one of his favourite paintings 'The Broken Windmill'.

Or, during a controversy about the new Arts Centre that was to be built on St Kilda-rd., of which Elliott was an opponent:

> I hear that you have sent to some Trustees long extracts about the Centre from my newspapers, but I haven't had them. Could you let me have a copy for my files?

Murdoch's intention was to get the best possible deal for the gallery. His correspondence covered a wide field of subject and recipient: Premiers of the State of Victoria, leaders of opposition parties, possible (and to him acceptable) aspirants for positions on the Gallery Trust, artists, architects, art critics and connoisseurs, antiquarians, art collectors and dealers, art gallery authorities and controllers in many parts of the world.

But the gallery trustees as a whole knew little of this. Some of them did, but they were the men he could trust, and whose appointment to the Trust he had, in most cases, sponsored; they were his loyal supporters. This was not the support of courtiers, for the men he persuaded to take a part in art gallery administrations were prominent in many fields of public, professional and commercial life: lawyers, doctors, newspaper editors, architects, merchants, artists or art lovers. Under his chairmanship was built bit by bit a body of experienced, intelligent, dedicated men. They were helping to strengthen the policy and administration of the National Gallery, and to build its image as a public institution.

Murdoch pushed ahead with his dream of an art and cultural centre in St Kilda-rd. on land occupied by Wirth's Circus. He badgered successive State Premiers about it and spelled out details of what it would look like in his newspapers. He was stirring interest in art as it had never been stirred before. In 1939 he inspired, and the *Herald* helped sponsor, an exhibition of contemporary French and English paintings in the Melbourne Town Hall. Basil Burdett had been dispatched to Europe and had collected a breathtaking selection of more than two hundred items of paintings and sculpture. There were pictures by Van Gogh, Braque, Utrillo, Pascin, Picasso, Vlaminck, Hodgkins, Sutherland, Dali and Cézanne. Such a show would have been a sensation anywhere in the world; to have secured it for Australia was a coup indeed for Murdoch. The then director of the National Gallery, J.S. MacDonald, was asked, in the euphoria of the moment, to report on nine paintings that had been marked as possible acquisitions for the gallery. He reported to a surprised Murdoch:

> They are exceedingly wretched paintings. Those who have followed up the career of the movement of which they are the material very well know that never in history has such a ramp as that which has forced them on the world, been engineered. We have seen the advertising efforts that have been made to urge us to swallow this putrid meat. We have been soused with one bucketful after another of jargon syphoned from Fry, Bell, Wilenski, Clutton-Brook, Freud, Jung and others - and used as if the pictures had to be boosted like a cheap line of socks. There is no doubt that the great majority of the work called 'modern' is the product of degenerates and perverts and that by the Press the public has been forcibly fed with it. As owners of a great van Eyck if we take a part by refusing to pollute our gallery with this filth, we shall render a service to art.

MacDonald was director of the gallery 1937-42. He had laid down in 1938 as a purchasing policy: 'We should have art without epoch, country, individual fashion, provided it is good art.' He also believed that only artists were competent to choose pictures. This was never accepted by the gallery trustees or the Felton Bequests Committee.

Murdoch disagreed with MacDonald's buying formulae. He believed that the needs of the gallery should be the guide, with quality a primary consideration. There should be, he declared, wide representation of periods, schools and artists necessary to make the gallery representative and to give it popular attraction and interest. The collection, he preached, must have variety, true educational value, and aim to be nationally important.

MacDonald's report was largely rejected by the trustees and by the Felton Bequests Committee. Two of the pictures were bought, 'Head of a Man' by Van Gogh and 'Dawn' by Felix Valotton. Murdoch believed it would be wrong to attempt to force any type of taste upon the people, but it would be right in every way to attempt to teach what is undoubtedly a teachable and a developing subject - appreciation of true beauty in art and architecture. Praising an artist he said: 'Communities owe a great deal to these thoroughly representative artistic men who have a much deeper influence than they are given credit for, because their works and their ideas spread, and we are indeed in daily touch with them in the most intimate way in our homes, if not from a picture on the wall, then from pictures and writings in our books.'

He believed in freedom of the artist. 'Art,' he said at one exhibition, 'must have a free soil. I myself whilst getting a great deal out of much that is called modern, can find nothing in the extremes. But I have friends who get satisfaction out of the strange designs of Braque and glory in Picasso. We certainly should not interfere with them. Let experiment and exploration in art always go forward. But the great workaday world needs the constant influence of the work that it can understand, and that is sincere, meaningful and competent.'

His general attitude to painting was homely; he liked to see *understandable* pictures in exhibitions, in galleries, in private houses. Yet he could and did recognise and applaud courage and enterprise in an artist. In opening the 1943 exhibition of Melbourne Contemporary Artists he remarked that it was 'a triumph over much unrecognition and conservatism and showed that we have made a lot of progress of late'. Its outstanding mark was that 'in refusing to paint externals, to reproduce smug correctness and conventional forms you have put good and penetrating thinking into what you have tried to paint'. He confessed that he was glad the group did not go into 'cubes and columns and many geometrical lines, because he could not follow those who convey their thoughts by this means ... These folk proclaim that they are at the door of the subconscious and the past and future worlds, but so far I have not been able to pass the language test!'

It was at this exhibition that he paid tribute to George Bell, 'the incorruptible teacher who has borne the torch' in Australia, and Rupert Bunny 'so fine and sensitive a colorist', and to Drysdale and Peter Purves Smith, 'those courageous young painters'.

The idea of a more specific attempt to educate the people in art than was then available always nagged at him. Could a teacher be found who could pass to students - and teachers - an appreciation of art that they could, in turn, pass on to more students and more teachers, so it would reach all the people ultimately? He talked it over with friends who agreed with him about the need, and the idea of a Chair of Arts at Melbourne University emerged. Daryl Lindsay probably had the inspiration first. He said that as there was no training ground in Australia for art scholars, there should be a Chair of Arts, and Melbourne University with the Melbourne National Gallery as a background for reference was the place for it. 'We talked it over; the idea was liked, and before we left my room it was called a Chair of Fine Arts. Murdoch said he thought he could get the directors of the *Herald* to take a part in it.'

The idea was further developed that night over dinner in the Melbourne Club, where they were joined by others. Sir Clive Fitts, a member of the Felton Bequests Committee, who was at this dinner party recalled Murdoch asking Medley how much money would be required to establish the Chair. Medley answered £40,000. Lindsay went on talking; Sir Clive watched Murdoch who was scribbling on a piece of paper held on his knee. He broke in on Lindsay and said, 'I'll ask the *Herald* if they'll put up the money.'

Murdoch put the idea to the directors of The Herald and Weekly Times and they agreed to sponsor the Chair. It would be known as the Herald Chair of Fine Arts. A first donation of £10,000 was made, and this was passed to the University of Melbourne on 29 September 1944. In the course of a covering letter Murdoch, as chairman of directors, said the money was to be applied 'for teaching the understanding and appreciation of the fine arts'. He added that the directors hoped to be able to build up that amount so that a Chair of Fine Arts could be established in the University.

A year later the *Herald* gift was increased to £30,000.

In late 1944 Lindsay was in England and met Joseph Burke - a private secretary to the then Prime Minister Clement Attlee - who he described as a serious, well-trained student of art history, one of the most promising art students of his generation. He asked Burke if he might put his name forward for the Chair. Murdoch began corresponding with him and soon afterwards the appointment was made. In April 1947 Burke was inaugurated in the Chair of Fine Arts for a three-year period. In June 1949 the University Council appointed Professor Burke to the Chair for life.

13 A very private battle

Sir Keith's 'retirement' message dictated to Miss Demello at Christmas 1949 had contained a warning that he would hardly be letting go the reins . . .

> I shall be much in the office as an active chairman of the company with, of course, the authority and control that emanates from the board. I shall always be glad to see employees, and hope to move around more than has been possible . . .
>
> In no sense can we relax or reduce any of our standards. We have to improve our products, extend our influence, increase our revenues and better our working lives. We have to examine everything we do, and see that it is modern in method and sound in result . . .

He made sure the outer limits of the *Herald* empire knew about his continuing presence and dropped a note in September of the following year to Douglas Brass in London:

> . . . moreover I have a medical report that although limiting in my work and activities, enables me to venture further in life with some assurances of being still useful. And the world needs us all just now - the world of press work particularly needs any good helpers.

He started flying about the world again to meet leaders, to argue about newsprint supplies, to attend Press Union conferences, often in severe storms that tossed the slow, piston-driven aircraft he had to use in countries like India to an alarming extent. He told his wife that though one plane was suddenly lurching groundwards 400 feet at a time, he was proud to say that he had not resorted to his digitalis tablets and had sometimes actually dropped off to sleep.

He wrote from New York: 'It's midnight. I'm writing this in bed, the room is not tidy but I'm getting through tomorrow. I worked hard at Montreal, two speeches, much negotiation and trouble but think I did well and have increased our newsprint allocation. Today: National City Bank for lunch; Associated Press afternoon; Fairfield Osborn for late afternoon; Swopes for dinner.'

He had two days in Washington, and wrote that he had had 'two wonderful days . . . I got only two minutes with the President, but half-hours with everyone else I wanted. They are most generous with their time and information. This country is at work fantastically, and the belief is that even now it could do so much damage to Russia that the Russians would do a lot to avoid general war. But by 1952 the destructive power will be simply colossal and by 1953 the Russian supply places could be continuously destroyed.'

Inside the *Herald* office very little had changed so far as Murdoch's role was concerned. He might not have been managing director any more, but anybody assuming 'K.M.' could be ignored when a big decision was being made would be greeted with a glare from the dark-brown eyes and a pout: 'I think I might suggest . . .'

But he was standing aside more during crises - the life-blood of a newspaper. When at early morning conferences Ron Hobbs, the laconic, asthmatic chief of staff, reported a Victorian town was being ringed by bushfires and a team of reporters and photographers was being rushed there, 'K.M.' might stroll into the glassed-in room on the third-floor afterwards and enquire from Hobbs details of what he was doing to cover the possible catastrophe. He would sit in on the leader-writing conference and sagely nod when points were brought up by Jack Williams, the managing editor, or leader writer, Frederick Howard. Whereas he had often virtually dictated leaders before, he now listened to the verbiage that began their construction.

He liked to be kept informed about a political row, ramming down his intercom lever and asking editor Archer Thomas how it was progressing. But he would otherwise keep out of it. 'On Saturday mornings,' said a colleague, 'he would come into his office and sit alone going through his mail. He seemed rather a lonely figure now.'

At midday during the week he might buzz Ralph Simmonds and suggest lunch at the Melbourne Club, which he had only joined ten years before he died. 'He had refused to join before that,' said Rupert Murdoch, 'because he wouldn't belong to a place in which he was going to be pressured. When he put up for it finally, it was at a time when he was confident that people would go to him for his opinion, rather than try and force theirs on him; which would have happened had he joined as a 40-year-old editor. At the same time, he was never an easy social person.'

His days were dawning more gently at home. Rupert recalled earlier breakfast scenes, with his father sitting up in bed at 6 am, the covers scattered with newspapers. Articles would be ringed; facts underlined; page margins filled with shorthand queries: why did not the *Sun* have that murder story the *Argus* made such play with? Why was the *Herald* final edition front-page last night such a mess? Who was that bright young writer the *Age* was featuring - could someone have a quiet word with him somewhere?

Now Sir Keith could have a leisurely breakfast in bed and glance through the papers without the sense of urgency that had been present before. He could eat his toast and marmalade and listen on his radio to the ABC news and feel, happily, that the crises were being grappled with under the eye of somebody else up on the third floor in Flinders-st. He would be going into the office, but as an observer rather than an interferer or referee.

That was the 'Herald Face' of Sir Keith Murdoch as the fifties began.

There was another, secret, disturbing Murdoch face that few of the outside world ever saw. It was known with some consternation by his wife, his children, his banker H.D. Giddy, and his accountant, Pat Ramsden.

He was worried about money. He had a massive overdraft, he was not 'liquid'; he was over-extended. Though he would never be financially embarrassed, his investment situation was not 'tidy'.

Albany Road, Toorak, the Murdoch's Melbourne home from 1946 until 1953. Weekends were invariably spent at Cruden Farm.

After so many tough years, brilliant years, building a newspaper empire, how could 'Australia's Northcliffe' have ever got himself into a position to be so concerned?

Simply he was anxious about the gamble he was involved with against death: whether his ailments would kill him before he could make his family 'secure for the future'. He often discussed it with Elisabeth after dinner at home, but the complexities of shareholdings, control and death duties were pushed into the background by her over-whelming feeling of injustice that her husband, a great man, was doing himself further damage at an age when most people could turn their backs on business burdens and enjoy life. Why could he not?

Murdoch had informed The Herald and Weekly Times board in 1948 that he was uneasy about the company continuing its monopoly of Adelaide newspapers; people were talking about it and not very kindly. He suggested that this should be undone; he put forward a proposition that the board should offer him - personally - the *News* shares held by the *Advertiser* and he would pay cash for them. He gave The Herald and Weekly Times a solemn undertaking - and put it in writing - that if the Murdoch family ever wanted to sell their Queensland Newspapers holding The Herald and Weekly Times would get first refusal.

He had - many years before - been advised that he should spread his investments rather than leave his eggs in one newspaper-constructed basket. So he became a 'Collins-st. farmer' and paid £6 an acre for 'Wantabadgery', a Riverina sheep property in 1938. But in 1946, when it was required for soldier settlement, he got only £7 an acre for it. He had then bought 'Booroomba', a part-leasehold, part-freehold property across the Murrumbidgee, south-east of Canberra, and was immediately cast into gloom by rabbits over-running the paddocks, floods that washed out the phalaris, and the immense task of clearing to make it workable. He complained to Rupert: 'The Government which has refused to revalue the pound is going to take 30 per cent of the wool cheques, and then take 13/6 in the pound out of the profits.'

Almost always present in his mind was the concern he had about what would happen to Elisabeth and the children after he died. Letters that survive in the vaults of banks and sharebroking firms illustrate his thirst for family financial impregnability. He gave orders to buy shares even at large premiums to gain firm control of News Ltd. and Queensland Newspapers, purchasing shares in both companies whenever they were offered and in any quantity available. All this was done with little thought to actual current values illustrated by company performance.

As late as 18 September 1952, *only sixteen days before he died*, he wrote to an Adelaide sharebroker saying he would give one shilling more than the market price of *News* shares and told him to buy up to 10,000. At that date he held 82,895 fully paid shares in Queensland Newspapers Ltd., but in order to pay for these he had had to ease out of his holdings elsewhere. He had, a few months earlier, been forced to get rid of 18,000 *Advertiser* shares, saying he 'owed a great deal to the bank'. Selling this scrip helped ease the pressure he had brought on himself by his heavy buying in Brisbane. It was a financial merry-go-round that he would have dearly loved to alight from, but could not.

He sold 17,000 *Advertiser* shares to The Herald and Weekly Times in September 1951: every penny he could raise was being channelled into News Ltd. He told Rupert in a letter he had 'a whale of a mortgage on Booroomba to help pay for *News* stock'.

How necessary was this race against time? Was he not comfortably off enough for his family never to worry?

'He was never trying to create a dynasty,' said Rupert, 'but he knew there would never be a place for me on the *Herald*, in which he held a paltry number of shares. I guess he wanted me to have an opportunity in journalism, in newspapers, and he said so in his will. I was a very untried, green boy of about nineteen.' While Rupert was at Oxford - studying politics, philosophy and economics - Sir Keith wrote to Douglas Brass: 'Thank you for being so kind to Rupert. He is serious-minded, and if he survives the pitfalls, will be a good, truth-telling newspaperman.'

Oddly, Sir Keith had given Rupert little actual advice about the profession he loved so dearly. It was discussed nightly at the table and Rupert was familiar with the problems, the personalities and the office disturbances. 'He didn't try to influence me at all. He had rather an indulgent attitude (even when Rupert joined the Labor Club). He liked me to work hard and I think tried to instil always into me the high, moral *purpose* of newspapers. We never had discussions about newspapers as a business; he never had anything much to say about the money the newspapers were making, or talked about advertising revenue - though of course Father understood the importance of this. He was one of the great *journalists* of all time, a great builder, a creator of solid foundations. He had a high-minded idea of what a newspaper could do in society.'

But he gave his son no *specific* advice? 'Oh (laughs),' he said, 'never trust Sydney newspaper proprietors.' Murdoch's dislike of the Sydney newspaper atmosphere was real enough. 'He came back from Sydney meetings mentally and morally exhausted,' recalled a colleague. 'But in spite of their "brigandage" the Sydney publishers usually accepted his leadership.'

There had been, up to nine months before his death, another heavy strain on the fibrillating heart, which had withstood so many years of stress.

Sir Keith was secretly planning - at 65 - a new business venture that would have dismayed the Australian newspaper industry. He was plotting to leave the *Herald* entirely, to buy the *Argus* and run it in opposition to the empire he had created.

The London *Daily Mirror* group had bought the *Argus* in 1949, but its efforts to inject Fleet-st. popular journalism into the Melbourne scene had not worked. It had used all the journalistic high-jinks of sensationalism, human interest and coloured ink, but the efforts were of no avail; the *Argus* was heavily losing money for the *Mirror* group and something had to be done.

Then a revolution took place in the pagoda-like *Mirror* building in Fetter-lane off Fleet-st., and it left Cecil King, a burly, shrewd fighter, as lord of the *Mirror* and its many publications. Murdoch was one of the first to cable congratulations on King's victory over his adversary Guy Bartholemew. King replied warmly and a correspondence between the two journalistic giants began. It was not long before they hatched a scheme . . .

Rupert Murdoch recalls the way it went. 'My father was fashioning a deal. He himself would leave the Melbourne *Herald* and would personally take over the *Argus*. He and King would put together a single organisation - Queensland Newspapers which he now controlled, the Adelaide *News*, which he partly controlled, and the *Argus*. The *Mirror*, for their part, would have to put a lot of money in. But it meant King could tell his board: "I have cured the whole problem; we will now have good management - and profits."' The Murdoch family would own 51 per cent of the new company - the goal that Sir Keith had long sought.

'It was risky for Dad financially. He was 65. And he was faced with having to borrow heavily to buy the rest of the Adelaide *News*. He cleaned himself out completely to buy the *News*. But the *Mirror* would be putting up cash as well as the *Argus*.'

Sir Keith fully realised the dismay people would feel when it was announced he no longer had anything to do with the *Herald*, when popular belief had always been that he owned the paper. He would now be fighting it tooth-and-nail as a rival.

'For a while, King was tempted. But in the end he came to the conclusion that he was risking too much, backing an old man whose health was dicey. Both of them - for their own reasons - pulled back from it. I think my father realised the people of Melbourne would never have believed he could leave the *Herald* of which he was so much a part; they might not accept what could possibly be seen as a breach of loyalty.'

So Sir Keith Murdoch had time again to tap out letters at home on the worn little Hermes he had always carried around the world; to get out his Hardy fly-rod and swish it around, readying himself for the trout season.

Then in April 1952 he was told he must go into hospital for a second prostate operation. He was operated on and remained in hospital until June. He was driven down to Cruden Farm to convalesce until he was strong enough to fly to Surfers Paradise with his wife.

Weeks after, he returned to the *Herald*, completely recovered from the operation, and he was given another thorough medical check. He came into his office beaming and told his private secretary, 'I have had a wonderful report from my doctors.'

Three days afterwards he presided at a morning meeting of the *Herald* board of directors. That afternoon he attended another meeting in his office. Next morning some papers and letters were taken to his house in Toorak.

Sir Keith was still in bed, writing to Anne, who was away at school.

> My beautiful and good Anne,
> A week has passed since I saw you in that famous game, which was as fast as league football. It was a good spectacle and all of us enjoyed it greatly.
> This has been a busy week and I am very tired. We spent last weekend at the farm and go down again today. Mum is doing too much but is in good form. We have had a splendid letter from Rupert and he is forgiven some of his misdemeanors. How did your studies go? Don't take matriculation lightly, old girl. You should probably concentrate on your weaker subjects now ... a tough month for you, because it will be pretty well all work, like my poor life.
> I have got four good Nolans for nothing because I sent him to the Northern Territory to illustrate some cattle articles ... [Referring to wool prices he had been paid for Wan-tabadgery wool, he remarked] We have to live on the smell of an oil rag and we are getting ready for good pensions.
> I am writing this in bed, but must arise now for many duties. I am going to work all the morning and play all the rest.

He and his wife went by car that afternoon to Cruden Farm to spend the weekend quietly. They walked about the garden and looked in at the farm buildings; he mentioned complete impending retirement and the improvements that would be made to the farm when that happened. He was relaxed, and happy. Any worries that he may have encountered during that week had passed from him. That evening - 4 October 1952 - he worked on his letters and then he and Elisabeth went to bed early.

Before he turned out the light that Saturday night Sir Keith said he believed he had finally achieved his goal; he could be free from worry. Said Dame Elisabeth: 'We were discussing a trip we had planned overseas. I remember so well Keith saying: "At last I can see daylight. It's all right. We *can* go, Lisa." He had got the bank overdraft down. He had been a little worried about what would happen if he had to go into hospital again; ... we were planning to attend the Coronation.'

Sir Keith died in his sleep during the night. The strong heart, over-worked for so long, could bear no more ...

Managing editor, John Williams, who had been for so many years Murdoch's right-hand man, wrote the *Herald's* leading article two days later. It said:

WE LOSE A LEADER

Today, for the first time in very many years, we take the leading column of the *Herald* to write about one of our own people.

By now, the death of Sir Keith Murdoch is known over most of the world. In our own country there have been warm and generous tributes. There have been appreciations, too, from statesmen, newspaper leaders and ordinary people in other countries in which Sir Keith and his work were known.

For his family and for his colleagues in newspaper work, these tributes are gratefully and respectfully acknowledged.

But today the people who work in this company may be forgiven if they take space to say that they feel in the death of Sir Keith a loss greater and more personal than could be felt in any other place outside his family.

It is the sort of loss that people can feel only after they have known someone for a very long time; known his strengths and his weaknesses; and on balance formed a judgment that is reflected in friendship, affection and respect.

Among the people who work in this company, Sir Keith Murdoch will always be remembered as a blend between an exacting employer and a good friend. His demand for exactness was exerted in all the things that he felt went to make a good newspaper - keen inquiry, close study of facts, clear writing and good production and, above all, sincerity of motive.

He found it hard to forgive shoddy work that reflected on the quality or standing of the newspapers, but never hard to forgive the honest man who was at fault. This office is full of legends of his sharp official condemnation of some piece of bad work, and full of his unofficial orders that the man or woman in question was to be treated kindly.

To those of us who have worked many years close to Sir Keith Murdoch in his creative work on our newspapers, it is hard to form an impartial judgment. It is doubly hard at a time like this when his loss means so much to so many.

But, even at this time of grief, we may be permitted to say that we feel we have been associated with a worthy newspaper achievement. We believe that we have seen created a newspaper structure that has striven in all its branches to serve the needs of this State and this Commonwealth and all its people.

We believe that, despite all the mass of human imperfections, this company of ours will continue to be served by men and women who will make a true attempt to tell the news honestly and soberly, to bring to the readers a proper appreciation of good community values, and a comment that will reflect the differing and conflicting views that can exist only in a democracy of free people.

A high standard of work has been set for us by Sir Keith Murdoch. We hope, in duty and modesty, that we shall not let that standard be diminished.

Epilogue

by Douglas Brass

Keith Murdoch was an Australian patriot of immense influence on affairs and tastes and standards over many years, a man of power who used power unblushingly, in half a dozen areas, a *believer* in his country and its capacities, an innovator, an enthusiast for quality in life and politics who died too soon to witness the surge of creative nationalism he and his papers had striven toward as a realisable dream.

This thread of fervent nationalism can be traced throughout his life. His ambitiousness, triggered perhaps by the challenge to overcome early physical, social and professional handicaps, and later nurtured by his Scottish pertinacity and the successes that bred success, was surely a major personal driving force. But increasingly, as the years went by, it became identified with his ambitiousness for his country. This was no narrow nationalism, blind to the nation's flaws or to the power and quality and good will of others. On the contrary, it was a pride in country that openly accommodated the security and tradition and progressiveness that powerful friends could strengthen in us by their friendship, alliance and example. With Murdoch it was always Australia first, right from the Gallipoli exercise to the obsessive anti-Communist phase. Home, family, city and country, these were the articles of faith.

But it could only be Australia first if certain conditions and obligations were accepted; and these were Australia's readiness to learn from others all the way from newspaper practice to appreciation of art to broad maturity of political thought and action, and Australia's acceptance of the duties as well as the benefits of membership of the English-speaking world as the price of the security that first Britain and then America was prepared to offer. Murdoch's agony in World War Two was his disappointment with Australia's national effort, and those five years took more out of him than even his family knew. In London and Washington he loyally pressed strenuous reassurances; but at home he and his papers were tireless advocates of greater national effort. His errors of judgment at the time can be traced directly to his knowledge of muddling and suspicions of half-heartedness in Canberra.

Murdoch then was passionately Australian, though broad-minded enough (through his upbringing, travels, connections and even tastes) to live his Australianism intelligently in an international context. Britain, though less to be trusted as time went on, had given us her civilised traditions, and in spite of her decline was to be cherished always for the things of the mind. America - and this was in line with the events and trends of his last fifteen years - was our strength, and her eccentricities were to be understood and even admired. Thus, even as the British connection was so obviously diminishing, Murdoch would continue to recharge his intellectual batteries in the company of Englishmen of quality and power; and thus, with a shrewd eye on the future, he would nurture his relationships with men of influence and talent in the United States.

Murdoch had not only his newspapers to pass on his knowledge and his message, though they were a pretty powerful medium when turned on at full blast with his candid and apt-to-be-lyrical prose. He had, as well, immediate access to the corridors of power, where prime ministers and their colleagues were his intimates - or enemies. He had made some of them, and unmade them, too. Lyons was but one example. But Murdoch was not so much a king-maker as a policy-maker. There was not the slightest tinge of personal spite in his make-up - and just as well for his peace of mind, considering some of the press proprietors and politicians he had to deal with. It was his big thinking, right or wrong, that guided his approach to a professional or national problem. What was best for Australia, in his reading of it, was the motivation of all his campaigning and politicising. If his methods at times raised eyebrows among the sensitive, as in the case of his emotional backing of Menzies' ill-fated anti-Communist bill or at the time of his over-zealous use of press powers at the Ministry of Information, it was patriotism that was at the heart of it and not wrongheadedness.

Perhaps, after all, Keith Murdoch died at the right time. This was the time of prosperity and security, the Menzies golden years and the end of the Cold War - and there were the beginnings of boredom and cynicism and intellectual revolt on all sides. What would Murdoch, and the papers that observed his old-fashioned standards, have done about sexual freedom, abortion, women's liberation, street riots, the lot? To say the least, he would have been unhappy; and in later years, like all men, he was not exactly flexible. And what would Keith Murdoch have done about Vietnam? Boots and all, in the interests of the American connection? Or the humaneness and the cautiousness that were always in him? One can only be certain that whichever way he moved it would have been wholeheartedly, and that his motivation as always would have been his reading of Australia's long-term interests.

Acknowledgements

Credit for the research background for much of this book must go to the late C.E. Sayers, who, before he died aged 77, prepared a 'life' of Sir Keith Murdoch which was unpublished. Sayers, a journalist, editor and noted historian, was a meticulous, painstaking gatherer of facts. It was he who discovered - enabling it to be published here for the first time - the full text of the Murdoch letter on the Dardanelles. Because of his own experience as a political reporter for the *Age* he was able to accurately set down the political scene of the Murdoch years.

For my part, I talked to the Murdoch family, and those who had worked for 'K.M.', who were able to bring his personality alive, recalling his mannerisms, his sensitivity, his kindnesses and his rarer toughness. Dame Elisabeth Murdoch gave me letters he had written to his father as he tramped Fleet-st. trying to get a job; (because I was there doing the same thing almost fifty years later I felt perhaps a little more keenly what he must have gone through). Mr Rupert Murdoch disclosed the shock move his father planned to make to the *Argus* just before he died.

In Canberra the Australian War Memorial Library kindly gave me complete access to the Bean Diaries which until then were to have remained closed until 1990; the National Library de-classified parts of the 1916-17 Royal Commission on the Dardanelles for me, and this allows us for the first time to read Murdoch's own spirited defence of his sensational letter.

I also consulted Cecil Edwards' book *The Editor Regrets* (Hill of Content Publishing Co., Melbourne, 1972).

I would also like to thank the Australian War Memorial, the BBC Hulton Picture Library, the National Library of Australia, the State Library of Victoria, and the Herald and Weekly Times for the photographs used in this book. Dame Elisabeth Murdoch supplied a wide range of family photographs.

My slim connection with Sir Keith Murdoch came when he employed me as a cadet reporter on the *Herald*, possibly the last reporter he interviewed personally for a position. We sipped tea that had been poured from a splendid silver tea service. Sir Keith glanced through my book of cuttings from the Albury *Border Morning Mail* and then closed the pages. 'Ahh ... good bush reporting,' he said. 'We must have a long talk some time.' I can almost hear him adding '... but not now'.

If Sayers and I have brought the memory of 'K.M.' a little closer to those who knew him, worked for him or loved him, both our jobs have been done.

DESMOND ZWAR
CAIRNS, 1980

126

Index